CHILD OUT OF TIME

GROWING UP WITH DOCTOR WHO IN THE WILDERNESS YEARS

HAYDEN GRIBBLE

Copyright © Hayden Gribble 2017

Cover illustration copyright © Paul Magrs 2017

All rights reserved

First edition 2017
Second edition 2017

The moral rights of the author have been asserted

The right of Hayden Gribble to be identified as the author of this work

has been asserted by him in accordance with the Copyright, Designs

and Patents Act 1988.

This book is sold subject to the condition that it shall not, by way of trade

or otherwise, be lent, resold, hired out or otherwise circulated without the

publisher's prior written consent in any form of binding or cover other than

that in which it is published and without a similar condition including this

condition being imposed on the subsequent purchaser.

ISBN 978-1-9998659-0-0

ISBN 978-1-9998659-1-7

Printed and bound by Ingramspark

www.haydengribble.net

In memory of my late father Alan Gribble, who put up with my Doctor Who obsession.

CONTENTS

FOREWORD BY ANDREW SMITH	9
PROLOGUE: AN END AND A BEGINNING	11
CHAPTER ONE: A MILD CURIOSITY	17
CHAPTER TWO: JAMES BOND IN SPACE	34
CHAPTER THREE: SILENCE IN THE LIBRARY	53
CHAPTER FOUR: ESCAPE TO DANGER	72
CHAPTER FIVE: THE FACT OF FICTION	93
CHAPTER SIX: THE CELESTIAL TOYROOM	111
CHAPTER SEVEN: DOCTOR WHO NIGHT	130
CHAPTER EIGHT: THERE'S NO POINT IN BEING GROWN UP IF YOU CAN'T BE CHILDISH SOMETIMES	148
CHAPTER NINE: REGENERATION	168
CHAPTER TEN: JARVIS COCKER IN SPACE	191
CHAPTER ELEVEN: FULL CIRCLE	203
ACKNOWLEGEMENTS	221
ABOUT THE AUTHOR	223

FOREWORD

I'm older than the *Doctor Who* TV series. Just. By a year and 4 months. I didn't have to discover it as Hayden did, simply because, throughout my childhood, it was just there. In the 1960s and 70s, for at least six months of the year, *Doctor Who* graced Saturday tea time on BBC1, and if you were a kid you watched it. It was our job. And who could resist that blend of adventure, sci-fi, monsters and heroism? We loved it, and we took it for granted it would always be there.

My first definite memory of watching the series is of seeing Yeti in the London Underground in early 1968 (if you're reading this you probably know that was the Patrick Troughton serial The Web of Fear). I was five years old.

I've felt lucky to have grown up experiencing classic *Doctor Who* as it was intended, in weekly episodic chunks with little or no knowledge of what was coming up. But reading Hayden's compelling account of his discovery of the series, I've been touched by this story of a different kind of appreciation, of 'discovering' the series.

This is a compelling personal story, and one that shows how the torch of support for *Doctor Who* has and will pass from one generation to another. It's also a vivid example of the strength of the concept behind the series, and its power to gather new aficionados.

Strap in and prepare to follow Hayden on his determined journey to enjoy and explore *Doctor Who* during the 'wilderness years'. The 1996 Paul McGann *The TV Movie* is the catalyst, followed by a chronological zigzag of stories and Doctors.

Whether you're an old fogey like me who watched the classic years as they went out, or you're of the 'wilderness years' generation, or among the new series fans, I know you'll be gripped by Hayden's story.

Andrew Smith

2017

PROLOGUE:
AN END AND A BEGINNING

It's hard to look back through the mists of time and remember absolutely everything from your past. Some things we choose to forget; others we can only recollect if we glance back through rose-tinted glasses, reflecting back another world that we used to inhabit. Sometimes, our imagination fills in the blanks, playing out like a movie in our heads where the explosions were bigger, the dialogue was more memorable and the romantic sub-plot now seems less important but still just as sad.

Memories tend to be foggy too on occasion. If we all think back to a specific moment in our lives, it's very hard to reconstruct absolutely everything as it was. People's faces may seem a little warped (much like Miss Evangelista in *Silence in the Library/Forest of the Dead*) or their voice is slightly different, and nothing is exactly how you remember it.

In short, the memory cheats.

CHILD OUT OF TIME

For me, though, I can honestly say that my childhood remains one of the easiest periods in my life to remember. One of my earliest obsessions - the thing that fuelled my fire as a little boy - was *Doctor Who*, the show that had adorned television screens across the globe for 26 years, inspiring generation upon generation of children and sending them scuttling into their Granny's bosom or – yes, I shall say it – behind the sofa. It had been watched by millions of fans, outgrown its standing on BBC One as the meat in between *Grandstand* and *Juke Box Jury* and become a British institution.

It's hard to think of a single child in the United Kingdom who had not heard of *Doctor Who*. Everybody knew what a Dalek was, what it sounded like and few had resisted the temptation to march around the school playground, exclaiming 'EXTERMINATE!' in a bid to ward away school bullies or nagging dinner ladies!

But then there were others who took their love for the show that little bit further. Those boys and girls who would sprint into their wardrobe and pretend it was a TARDIS, or sit inside a stuffy classroom drawing pictures of the Doctor battling his fiercest enemies whilst wondering which Target novelisation to read when they got home.

Everyone has their favourite Doctor - and they are theirs to keep for all of eternity. Whether it's William Hartnell - the crotchety old man with the twinkle in his eyes; Patrick Troughton - the Beatle-haired cosmic hobo; Jon Pertwee - the man of action in the sort of frilly shirt Jimi Hendrix would have been proud of; Tom Baker - whose impossibly long scarf and wide toothy grin mesmerised all; Peter Davison - the dashing young older brother; Colin Baker - the brash, multi-coloured bachelor of the Universe; Sylvester McCoy - the funny man with the "?" umbrella and steel in his eyes; Paul McGann - the handsome, Byronesque romantic; Christopher Eccleston - the leather-jacketed Northerner with survivor's guilt; David Tennant - the nerd in the pin-stripped suit who gave a face to "geek chic"; Matt Smith - with his foppish hair and manifesto to make bow ties cool again; or the latest incumbent in the role, Peter Capaldi, whose stern yet highly likeable Time Lord has captivated audiences all around the world. And now we have Jodie Whittaker, the first female to take on the role, ready to step into the TARDIS and take us on new adventures. In one way or another, we've all looked up to them.

In whatever shape or form, the Doctor has always been a bit like a surrogate parent, although he wouldn't bother taking you on boring trips to the zoo! He takes us to the most imaginative, exotic and dangerous places we could only dream of.

From the time of the Caveman 100,000 years BC to the year 5 billion, we have travelled with him to Telos, Karn, Gallifrey, Vulcan, Metebelis 3, Androzani Minor and Skaro.

He has taken us back in time to meet Marco Polo on a Journey to Cathay, save Madame de Pompadour from clockwork robots, help William Shakespeare defeat a trio of witch-like creatures and even give Vincent van Gogh a heart-warming glimpse into the future.

We have even seen him redeem an earlier, secret incarnation of himself from resolving the Time War with genocide on his darkest day. With the TARDIS, his Police Box-shaped, "dimensionally-transcendental" (bigger on the inside!) time and spacecraft, the galaxy is his oyster and, week after week, we joined him for the trip of a lifetime.

But for 16 years, there were no adventures. Well, not on television in any case. At the conclusion of the third part of *Survival* on the 6th December 1989, *Doctor Who* ended.

Yet the death of the Doctor had been plotted a long time before then. In the face of accusations of poor production values, weak scripts, tepid acting and a Head of BBC TV who publicly hated it, the show nearly finished in 1985.

However, it had limped on and had started to get back on its feet by the late 1980s, when long-serving producer John Nathan-Turner was re-invigorated by the arrival of a new and youthful script editor, Andrew Cartmel, and a darker, more mysterious Seventh Doctor as played by McCoy.

Tighter scripts, a more realistic and believable companion in the form of Ace played by Sophie Aldred and an allusion to the fact that the Doctor was not all that he seemed led to a huge upturn in quality for the 26-year-old show.

Despite this, *Doctor Who* was still frowned upon by the BBC, who had scheduled it opposite another long-running British institution, the ITV soap *Coronation Street*.

The belief held by those on the sixth floor of BBC Television Centre was that no-one was prepared to take it on and give it the love that it really needed. It seemed like there was no confidence in *Doctor Who* now and, with viewing figures down and interest from the general public seemingly almost non-existent, the writing was on the wall.

The final story to be recorded in the classic series' run, *Ghost Light*, wrapped in August 1989, with no word on whether the show would be returning. Four months later, as the Doctor and Ace walked off our TV screens towards pastures new, the show quietly and almost apologetically disappeared.

It was during that long, hot summer that - around the same time that the production team would have been putting together the final plans for location OB recording on *Survival* - at 9.30pm on June 8th, I was born in Cambridge.

CHILD OUT OF TIME

Just two days later, the cast and crew began recording the story that brought down the curtain on 26 years of adventures in space and time.

An end and a beginning…

For the first time since its inception, *Doctor Who* was off the air with next to no possibility of making a comeback.

From that time, children stopped jumping into their wardrobes on the run from imaginary Cybermen, drawing Daleks in class or picking up Target novelisations.

There was no longer a hero, a champion for the outcasts who struggled to fit in. It was as though he had walked into his TARDIS and set his controls for dematerialisation, never to return: a whole generation lost to the powers of Science Fiction's greatest creation.

It was in this Doctor-less world that I grew up.

This is the story of how one little boy would try to find the Doctor in any way, shape or form and the obstacles he faced in doing so.

This is the story of growing up without *Doctor Who* in the Wilderness Years…and how I lived through it.

CHAPTER ONE:
A MILD CURIOSITY

'Quick, draw the curtains, it's starting!'

My mum was urging my dad to shut out the dying light from our little family room at the Travelodge. She was keen to create as much tension and atmosphere as she could for me and my little sister who, although just three at the time, looked fascinated by the chaos surrounding her.

I remember the underlying excitement that both my parents were displaying and the feeling that something very unique was about to happen.

I, on the other hand, was feeling very tired. The events which had led to that evening on the 27th May 1996 had absolutely nothing to do with my first moment of exposure to *Doctor Who*. In fact, it had all been a little boring for this usually-excitable, soon-to-be seven-year-old.

It had all started with a mad dash up the M6 to the Midlands to see my mother's extended relatives. We did this quite a lot in my childhood, travelling at the crack of dawn, rock-like sleep dust still stuck to the corner of my eyes, being jolted along in our old, faded red Vauxhall Cavalier while trying to slumber on my welcoming Captain Scarlet pillow.

However, on that Saturday something was to change my life forever. And like many things, it hasn't been until now that I have come to realise just how important this was to prove for me and the direction I would pursue as an adult.

Upon visiting my great-grandmother at a nursing home in Warwick, my eyes darted around her little flat in the vain hope that there would be something (anything!) to do. I wanted to occupy my mind whilst my parents were talking grown-up things with my mum's aunt as Great-Nan Summerton sat in her chair, watching them chatter away.

Suddenly, out of the corner of my eye, I noticed a magazine resting untouched on the wooden coffee table.

It was that week's *Radio Times* and, like a child who sees a toy he wants to get his grubby hands on before another boy or girl gets to it, I snatched it up. I turned it over and saw that brilliant cover for the very first time: 'It's time to return...DOCTOR WHO - THE MOVIE.'

The picture showed an Edwardian-looking man with a pocket watch in his hand and what seemed to be a column of beautiful sapphire-like crystals to his right, which bewildered me.

How could these two things, a man with old fashioned dress-sense accompanied by something so futuristic, merge together so convincingly in my imagination?

I had to find out more. I flicked open the magazine, feeling the weight of something else, smaller than the publication itself, entombed within the pages. Now, in my mind's eye, the look on my face resembled that of Indiana Jones in *Raiders of the Lost Ark* when he discovers the golden idol in the temple.

In reality, it probably didn't, but I like to think that was my expression. Before me was a smaller pull-out supplement, adorned with the faces of eight very different-looking men. Their heads floating in a line through the enchanting vacuum of space, each one with the look of a man you could trust, whose eccentricities and other-worldliness intrigued me.

My dad must have spotted what I was looking at as he towered above me. 'Oh, *Doctor Who*,' he observed. I craned my neck to look at him.
'Which one is *Doctor Who*?' I asked.
'All of them.'
'All of them?!' What did he mean? Those three words blew my young mind. All of these men were the same person?! How could this be? They were all so different.

None of them bore any resemblance to the one that preceded or followed the other. Some of them looked old; maybe they were the same age as my Grandad? One of them looked like he was only just older than me, with very blonde hair barely concealed by a cream-coloured hat.

Two of the faces were in black and white and that confused me even further. Why were they not in colour like all the rest? But the picture which baffled me even more was that of a blue box that sat in the middle of this intriguing cascade of faces. It had the words 'Police Public Call Box' painted along its top and two doors with a little panel in a different shade of blue with writing far too small for my eyes.

I turned to the front of this pull-out again and the words 'RETURN OF THE TIME LORD' struck me. What's a Time Lord? A torrent of questions flooded my brain. I wanted answers. Tentatively, I opened the magazine.

I don't remember reading many of the words in the articles. In fact, I skipped past the opening couple of pages that concentrated on *The TV Movie*, whatever one of those was. I was just absorbed by the facts on who this man (or men) was.

The first page I glanced on properly concerned a man called William Hartnell. The picture of him, craning his neck and looking off into the far distance, looked both ancient and forever at the same time. I thought he must be over a hundred years old as the picture had browned but even in this sepia-toned snapshot there was something scary yet reassuring in his face.

On the following page, a kinder-looking, almost silly man stood out, wearing a very tall hat and resting his head on what looked like a rock. I liked him instantly.

Someone or something must have disturbed my wonder because I then remember putting the magazine down and running off to play. But whilst I sat there pretending that my *Action Man* was going out with *Barbie* at the behest of my sister, I remember looking over to the half-open *Radio Times* calling for my attention. Happily, my great-grandmother allowed me to rip the pull-out away from the magazine and keep it. Even now, I recall the wonder I found within those pages as I gleefully pored over the pictures and text.

But this had not been my first interaction with *Doctor Who*.

As a toddler, I can remember being plonked in the play-pen of a hospital waiting room, peering up and seeing strange, black-and-white images flickering from a television high above my head. I have no memory as to why we were at a hospital - it could have been around the same time that my mother was pregnant with my sister. Fast forward a year or two and again I was gaping up at a TV screen.

CHILD OUT OF TIME

This time there appeared to be a white-haired man in a costume that I remember thinking looked like something you'd wear at Halloween, being accosted by Morris-dancers. 'How odd,' I thought.

Of course, twenty-odd years down the line, I now know that this was a BBC2 repeat of the Jon Pertwee classic *The Daemons* but back then it was yet another tiny moment in a world so big and confusing that it passed into insignificance.

The first time I was made vaguely aware that there was a programme called *Doctor Who* was in the build-up to the BBC's 1993 *Children in Need* charity telethon. Once again, it was Jon Pertwee who stood out more prominently than anybody else.

His look was so majestic, so outlandish, like that of a dandy. I watched lying on my belly on my parents' bed, chin in hands as he gate-crashed *Noel Edmonds House Party.*

He was very funny-looking; his bouffant white hair reminded me of that an old school dinner lady, but there was something totally reassuring and trusting in his face.

I vaguely recall my mother yelping and propelling herself upwards into a sitting position on the bed. I turned to face her as she handed me a pair of 3-D glasses. I had moaned all evening about how they didn't work, how nothing stood out on the TV and that all they did was turn one eye red and the other green. Nonetheless, I was unaware that I was to witness the triumphant return of the Doctor...

Sadly, as we all know, it was not the triumphant return that many would have hoped for. *Dimensions in Time* (or *Doctor Who meets EastEnders* as I like to call it) was universally panned, with only the odd die-hard fan to defend it. The marriage between Britain's favourite Time Lord and the East End setting of Walford was convoluted, disappointing and above all silly - even in this four-year-old's eyes!

Alas, this little excursion into the strange, new world of *Doctor Who* didn't spark a desire to learn more about the Doctor, his companions and his gallery of enemies.

Yet just three years later, roughly 200 miles away and now only slightly more aware of this magical world and its treasures and trappings, that spark was ignited. The room was dark and moody; the light of the small television between two cream wardrobes was the only beacon shining out to us.

We all hushed ourselves as I put the *Radio Times* pull-out away like a student putting his revision back in his bag before an exam. The announcer's voice boomed through the tiny speaker grille: 'Now on BBC1...he's back...and it's about time...!'

My anticipation had reached fever pitch. My heart was beating so fast it could have broken clean through my rib cage and I wouldn't have noticed! Here it was, my first ever PROPER *Doctor Who* - my first ever Doctor. The tension and excitement was palpable.

And then, a solemn caption bled into shot: 'Dedicated to the memory of Jon Pertwee – 1919 – 1996'

Well, that didn't half dampen the mood for a second or two. Jon Pertwee - the only Doctor I had fleeting memories of through that *Children in Need* skit and that brief memory of him trying to flee a band of overzealous Morris dancers - was dead. I didn't know. How could I? I had only known of the show's true existence for a couple of days. Death, though still hard to comprehend even now, is a foreign concept when you're nearly seven. I just remember thinking how sad it was that he would never get to see *Doctor Who*'s triumphant return to our screens.

As the brilliant red of Skaro honed into view, my mind was scrambled by the back story that was hitting me in the face. Who is the Master? What is a Dalek? Aren't they those things the older boys at school used to mimic with baskets on their heads?

Suddenly, those wonderful, awe-inspiring first few bars filled the room and that brilliant blue logo, proudly igniting the starry darkness of space shot through the screen. I was immersed, my pulse throbbing to the tune of the music that was now flowing into my ears. It was one of the most thrilling and gorgeous pieces of music I had ever heard.

Instantly, I wanted to hum it and tap out the rhythm of four out with my fingers on the edge of the bed. It was like I had been hypnotised by the drumming in the Master's head eleven years too early!

As the blue box hurtled towards the screen, I could feel my body being drawn towards it, like I was being carried closer and closer to the television in some ethereal way.

I was *in* the adventure! Everything else - my mum, my dad, my curiously quiet little sister, that room in the Travelodge - they all ebbed away and I was following the Doctor's footsteps. I felt like I was standing by his side as the TARDIS ('Oh, so *that's* the blue box's name!' I called out) spiralled out of control. I was in the operating theatre as his seventh life was prematurely ended by that stupid woman in the flowing dress. I was in Bruce's bedroom (the ambulance driver) as that weird, translucent snake propelled itself down his oesophagus (yes, it was awkward and I didn't know where to look…). I wasn't just in the adventure…I was LIVING it!

And then, of course, there was the regeneration.

Looking back, many fans and commentators have lamented *The TV Movie* for being too continuity-ridden, too complex and too concerned about its own importance to bring the show back successfully after its seven-year-long hiatus.

All of that is easy to say in hindsight, but all of those opinions pale into insignificance when you are a child watching it for the very first time. For me then, it was a perfect crash-course in all that was great and good about *Doctor Who*. It explained to me that the Doctor could regenerate up to twelve times, completely change his appearance and renew himself at the point of death.

It taught me that his greatest nemesis was a villain called the Master, who originated from the Doctor's home planet of Gallifrey, which was also heavily mentioned throughout the story.

It briefly alluded to the Daleks, who I had seen pictures of throughout my childhood but had never associated with being a part of *Doctor Who* folklore. Truth be told, I thought they were something to do with *Star Wars*, but I couldn't be sure because I hadn't seen that either. And then there was the TARDIS. That blue police box, so incongruous to its surroundings in downtown San Francisco. I'd even learnt what the acronym stood for: Time and Relative Dimension in Space.

I can remember the anticipation of witnessing my very first regeneration. It was hard not to suppress the excitement and, as the *Radio Times* pull-out had made clear, it was something that had always happened in *Doctor Who*. Both my parents had done their best to explain how it happened

('Basically, another actor comes in and plays the part, only he is totally different to the last one…Hayden, are you following this?'). But listening to their memories of watching the Doctor change (I learnt later that my dad remembers watching William Hartnell transform into Patrick Troughton at the conclusion of *The Tenth Planet* way back in 1966 as clear as day!) prepared me little for my first experience of the greatest piece of plot expediency in TV history.

Truth be told, I had actually grown rather fond of Sylvester McCoy in those few scenes he had as the ill-fated Seventh Doctor. I don't think I was quite prepared for him to be killed so cruelly at the hands of Dr Grace Holloway. In fact, I didn't like her for the rest of the episode as she had effectively killed the Doctor.

So, as McCoy's features gurned into those of Paul McGann, I felt a twinge of cosmic pathos. However, it didn't take long to become totally captivated by the vibrant Eighth Doctor.

As for the Master, well, he was a different kettle of fish altogether. I couldn't work him out. One minute he was dark, foreboding and as menacing as the worst school bully imaginable. Then, by the end, he had turned into a sort of Kenneth Williams impersonation! I'd already seen a glut of *Carry On* films on many a rainy weekend at my Grandparents' house. His character bamboozled my already confused mind.

I don't remember following much of the plot - it was a little too convoluted for my young brain to compute. It wasn't analytical enough to work out what a beryllium atomic clock was and how it was going to save the universe. I was unsure what the Eye of Harmony was or why the Doctor had it aboard his magical spaceship.

The kiss between Grace and the Doctor brought an audible grunt of disapproval from one of my parents who didn't seem to be enjoying what they were watching. I didn't find that particular moment very pleasing either. I was still at that age when any kiss, even from your Granny, was an icky incident. But, judging from the reaction from my mother and father, this was something the Doctor did not do often - or at all!

There were some endearing moments that kept this little boy engaged with the story. I really liked Chang Lee, who had accidentally caused the old Doctor to get shot when he landed in the wrong place at the wrong time during a gang fight. I didn't know if I was supposed to like the guy or not but I found him oddly engaging. After all, like Grace, he had played a part in my hero's downfall and he even teamed up with the Master! Maybe it was his redemption at the end that won me over.

But looking back, I find it odd how the Doctor really is surrounded by people who have either had a role in his death or are out to kill him again. The Master's torture contraption that he makes the

Doctor wear was a little too much for me, if I'm honest. Plus I found the *The TV Movie* to be too long.

It was hard to keep fully engaged with the plot as I grew more tired and I didn't feel like I had time to get to know the new Doctor at all. It seemed like he'd only been in it for half an hour, whatever half an hour felt like - my time-keeping was rather poor back then (some would argue, it still is now!)

By the end of *The TV Movie*, it was getting quite late and my eyelids were starting to feel heavy. As the song *'In A Dream'* played over the TARDIS drifting away into space, my dad must have spotted my head drooping and he sprang up to turn the TV off.

'Well, can't see it coming back after that!' he muttered. Clearly, my father was not overawed by what he had seen.

'Will it be on again next week?' I asked as I rolled off my parents' bed and into my own.

'Nope. That was a one-off,' was my father's reply.

'We can always check in the paper next week if you like. Remember, they've also got that new comic strip in the *Radio Times* too,' my mum chirped in optimistically.

My face fell. So, that was it?! No more *Doctor Who*?! That's not fair!

That night, as I lay on the pull-out bed under the window of the Travelodge room, I had a chance to mull over what I had seen. I had liked the Doctor - both of them - and wanted to continue watching the Time Lord's adventures. But if what my parents said was true, then how? It seemed really cruel to give something so rich in adventure, fun and appeal to a highly impressionable boy and then snatch it away again.

It reminded me of those occasions when I was allowed to watch my cousin play on the Sega Megadrive but never to play on it myself.

This show had only been in my life for a couple of days but already I was hooked. I remember going back to school the next week and speaking to my friends about it. I had asked them if they had seen *Doctor Who* and if they liked it. Depressingly, none of them had, although I did develop a new-found respect for my best friend Robin, who knew what the Daleks were.

But this nugget of appreciation for something that had been dead for all our lives did little to stir any interest in our little class at Steeple Bumpstead Primary School. Fairly soon after that, my own interest dwindled a little. I had no outlet, after all. No videos, no books, no TV series to watch.

Even my seventh birthday had come and gone. As I tore into the wrapping paper, salivating over the presents beneath, not one of them had anything to do with the show. All I had was that glorious pull-out, but that soon found its way into the drawer as I felt it taunted me. For a while at least, my enthusiasm perished.

Then there came a truly memorable day one July morning. Memorable for all of the wrong reasons.

It was Sports Day and it was mandatory to take part. Even though my only sporting interest was in football at this time, I was due to run in the 50-metre race, despite the fact that I run like a penguin with its arse on fire! I also wanted to get my own back on my friend, Andrew, who had impeded my lane in the same race the previous year, leading me to burst into tears.

This time I did pretty well - I think I finished fourth - and was walking over to my house team when I was brought crashing to the floor by a sudden, sharp pain in the top of my thigh. I cried out in agony and fell on the floor. My teacher ran over as did some of my friends to see what the matter was. I don't recall what happened next or the sequence of events, but it led me to have an operation, a stay on the children's ward for a day or two and then a week at home with my leg up.

It was during this stay at home that *Doctor Who* was to plant itself permanently in my life.

I had spent most of that day plumped up on the sofa, watching children's TV interspersed with stuff my mum wanted to watch like *Neighbours* and *This Morning*. I was bored to tears by the tedium of being stuck at home instead of running around like I usually did so, when the doorbell rang, I limped to see who it was, despite my mother's plea to stay lying down. Fat chance! Anyway, it could have been a friend and I was so bored I was desperate to talk to anyone!

It was my friend, Nathan, who lived just down the road from my parent's semi-detached house in the Essex village of Steeple Bumpstead. He had brought me a Get Well Soon card that everyone in my Year 2 class had contributed to.

In little square panels, each of them had drawn a picture of something I liked. As I whimpered back onto the sofa, I held the card (which was roughly a metre in height!) and smiled as my mum pointed out what was drawn on the front.

There, in the middle of the collage, was a child's visual interpretation of the TARDIS! It stood out proudly in the correct shade of blue with the words POLICE BOX dominant across its top.

I forget which of my classmates had drawn it, but their attention to detail was incredible. The snowflakes included in the picture were another matter, resembling the size of bowling balls, but given that my classmates were seven at the time, I can forgive them that small discrepancy. However, this little picture was to play a pivotal part in my first, tentative steps into becoming a full-blown fan of the show.

I dug the *Radio Times* magazine out from the drawer again and studied it. I looked at the number of episodes I had to catch up on and made it my goal there and then to watch them and these older, wonderful Doctors.

The mini-hiatus was over, the two months that had passed since *The TV Movie* was broadcast now seemed like two minutes. *Doctor Who* was in my life again…and, this time, I wasn't going to let him go away again!

CHAPTER TWO
JAMES BOND IN SPACE

A week, in the mind of a child, can feel like an eternity. Luckily for me, it was passing in the blink of an eye. As I continued to recover from my operation, I was delighted by my first *Doctor Who* related present. The card had gone a long way to quenching my thirst for more things *Who*. But, before I go any further, I want to tell you a little more about that week.

My grandparents had spent that Saturday morning travelling from Clacton-on-Sea in Essex to see how I was getting on. As upsetting and confusing as an operation can be for a child, even one as minor as mine, it hardly affected me because my parents had kept me well occupied. In fact, it had all been like a very surreal adventure. Going to hospital and waking up in a ward full of children my age, although I was bed-bound and unable to take part in any games, as new and strange as it was, didn't faze me one little bit.

One of the strongest memories I have of my stay was a boy, not much older than me, who was staying in the hospital bed next to me. The unfortunate lad had accidentally knocked a kettle full of boiling water over his head at home and was scheduled to have skin graft surgery. His injuries were appalling. I enjoyed playing with him, and sympathised with him regarding his terrible wounds. I once put my hand under the boiling water my dad was putting in our paddling pool and suffered the consequences, going on to miss out on an afternoon of sitting in the sun as I was soaking my scalded hand in the downstairs sink.

My mother, who stayed overnight with me, thought I'd possibly be scared of his disfigurement. But nothing made me feel scared or nervous. In fact, I was pretty fearless as a kid.

An added bonus of being in hospital was that it was great to be fussed over for once. Numerous nurses tended to my every whim. They were all very pretty and caring and I couldn't help returning their bright smiles. I recalled my mum telling me that when I was born, the nurses had affectionately nicknamed me 'Scrappy' on account of my small frame and messy, thick baby hair and that, on more than one occasion, she discovered, upon visiting me in my cot, that a nurse had already beaten her to it and was cradling me in an armchair.

Ever since my sister had been born, of course, I hadn't really held as much attention as I had enjoyed before. So, for the first time in two years, I was numero uno in people's books again. And I sucked up the attention like it was a refreshing glass of cola gushing through a silly straw.

Naturally though, there was only so much that could occupy me. I'd grown tired of our collection of Disney films and my Mum's appalling daytime TV schedule held no interest for me. I was becoming one of the most dangerous things a seven year old boy can be – bored.

But that visit from Nan and Grandad soon had me chirping again. I'd have bounced around the living room like Tigger at their arrival just to see two familiar-friendly faces.

After giving them the biggest hug my puny arms could muster as a reward for their sympathy and concern, they presented me with a gift. As I removed the rogue fluff that had fallen from the trim on my Nan's coat and stuck to my face, I gazed upon what looked like a VHS cassette.

Longing to know what lay in wait inside, I tore away the wrapping paper. It was indeed a video. But this wasn't just any gift. It was a *Doctor Who* video.

I literally gasped. A *Doctor Who* episode – for me! I didn't know what to say. It was like all my prayers had been answered. Finally, after the months that had passed since that fateful day in May when *The TV Movie* and that *Radio Times* pull-out had time crashed into my little world, I was about to watch my very first old, PROPER *Doctor Who* story. It wasn't a stone-cold classic. There were no Daleks or Cybermen. I knew nothing about it. I'd never even heard of the story. It wasn't mentioned in my *Radio Times* pull-out.

This was a mystery wrapped in plastic. To my Grandparents, it was just an ordinary *Doctor Who* story. Not for long. The 1983 adventure, *Snakedance*, was about to find such a special place in my heart that, even today, the mere thought of it transports me back to that first, wonderful viewing

I analysed the front cover like a detective looking for a clue in a crime scene. The first thing that drew my attention was the logo. It looked very familiar, with the title of the show in the diamond shape from the Tom Baker title sequence. Not that I'd even seen it yet, but I did remember it from its inclusion in the pull-out magazine

Yet, looking at the painting, it didn't take a newly-awakened novice like me to realise that the man adorning the cover was not Tom Baker. It was a young man, with what to my eyes looked like slightly grey hair. He was wearing a beige, yellowish coat and had what looked like a stick of celery pinned to his lapel. I asked my dad to go and get the pull-out for me so that I could work out which Doctor this was. I couldn't for the life of me remember if it was the Third or the even the Sixth.

'You know who that one is, it's Peter Davison!' a helpful observer said. Of course! The Fifth Doctor. From what I'd read, he was the youngest of all the Doctors so far. I couldn't wait to see him. I was full of questions in the build-up to that first watch. How different will he be to Paul McGann? Will he be funny? How will he deal with that snake?

I mainly remember two things sticking out from that front cover. One was the poisonous drool that lingered on the protruding teeth of the giant snake which seemed to be hissing into the Doctor's ear. In my head, that was why he looked rather glum! The other was the two attractive girls. Who were they? Were these the Fifth Doctor's companions? What were their names?

In my haste to bundle it into the video player, I dropped the cassette and read the blurb on the back. The synopsis raised yet more questions. Who's Tegan? Where's Manusa? What's a Sumaran Empire? And what confused me even more was the writer's name - Christopher Bailey. That was the name of my friend's dad! I had no idea he'd written a *Doctor Who* episode.

The inner sleeve treated me to a collage of other *Doctor Who* videos available to buy. I don't recall all of the stories on offer but I do remember my grandad telling me that they nearly bought *Arc of Infinity*. A close shave. If that had been my first story, my fanatical devotion to *Doctor Who* may have been short lived indeed!

Apart from the strange amalgamation of images on the cover, I stumbled into this one blind. I had only seen one *Doctor Who* episode before now and all this series was doing was confusing me. But that only increased my excitement to have all my questions answered.

According to my parents, it would be rude to ignore guests. I thought it was even ruder not to watch the present they had bought me! Maybe my family hadn't been bitten by the *Doctor Who* bug like I had.

Later that afternoon, as soon as my Grandparents had gone home, I went over to the video player and put the cassette in. Despite my injury, I jumped back onto the sofa with all the grace of a boy cannonballing into a swimming pool.

'Careful!' Mum winced, but I was taking no notice. The screen went blank. Expecting *The TV Movie* title sequence and music arrangement, I was startled by the old BBC video ident that I used to find slightly creepy. Then, with a screech, I was greeted by a star field hurtling towards me accompanied by an electronic score.

I found this arrangement odd. This wasn't the beginning to *Doctor Who* I had expected. Did that mean that the music, like the titles, was different for every Doctor? I didn't care much though. I was loving it! As the music took a higher pitch, a face broke through the collection of stars and the pleasant, open face of Peter Davison welcomed me into this strange world.

CHILD OUT OF TIME

As soon as the words, *DOCTOR WHO* organised themselves, I was in the moment. Everything else melted away again, just like that evening in the Travelodge a couple of months before.

Although it is not highly regarded by fans in general, *Snakedance* was an engaging and entertaining debut story for me and I love it to this day. I'm not sure that I had the foggiest what was going on, but this Fifth Doctor was fun, serious, silly, authoritative, intelligent and always the outsider.

He behaved differently to everyone else in the story and always seemed one step ahead of the other characters who struck me as being a little dim, especially John Carson's delightful interpretation of the archaeologist Ambril (even when he was oblivious to the reason for the missing face on the Six Faces of Delusion). I felt like I, the viewer, was one step ahead along with the Doctor and his very pretty companion Nyssa and, in a way, I felt rewarded as this was clearly a show that was not talking down to its audience.

I was further comforted by a familiar face in this sea of cosmic mystery. Although I didn't know his name then, I had seen Martin Clunes in *Men Behaving Badly* (being the oldest means you get to watch a lot of telly with the grown-ups!) yet I found his brattish portrayal of Lon summed up many a school bully I had come to know in my time.

In fact, the scene in which a possessed Tegan and Lon show Ambril to a cave of lost Sumaran treasures and proceed to break them in a bid to manipulate him was shockingly close to home. I remember having a toy broken by a boy a couple of years above me in a futile gesture of superiority that ultimately did nothing but win him a detention at lunchtime. I was hoping the Doctor was going to impose a similar punishment on Lon at the end!

The theme of possession and loss of control ran true throughout *Snakedance*. Janet Fielding's performance as Tegan was spell-binding and she quickly became my favourite companion...for the time being! Obviously, I hadn't seen *Kinda* yet so I had no background knowledge of why or what took control of Tegan there, or what it even looked like.

There were little hints to a far greater back story. It was like watching the original *Star Wars* trilogy in reverse! I actually did start my *Star Wars* odyssey by watching *Return of the Jedi* first and working my way back, but that's a story for another time. Tegan bewitched me. She seemed far more interesting than Nyssa, although I think I fancied Sarah Sutton a little more. But, when she's talking in her sleep to the Doctor in Part One and regresses back to a six-year-old in her garden, I felt a sudden tingle of apprehension scuttle up my spine. It was the first time that I felt the sense of fear that *Doctor Who* could bring.

Yet I didn't duck for cover behind a cushion or dive behind the sofa. No! It engaged me and pulled me further into the story.

By the time she's fully under the control of the mysterious Mara and summoning up that hideous skull from inside the crystal ball, I was gripped. That synth build-up from Peter Howell, the blood curdling scream from Hilary Sesta's petrified fortune teller, the screech that accompanied the shattering of the ball as the terrifying Mara pierced through…and then the credits. What a pulsating end to what is still for me the most effective and atypical cliffhanger in *Doctor Who* history.

'Oh, that's all I remember from those cliffhangers,' my mum said as she sat watching it with me that Saturday afternoon. 'The women always screamed at the end.'

'Really? Well that's because they are frightened,' I replied.

'Yes, but you'd never see the Doctor scream like that,' she retorted. 'It was always the women.'

I had no idea what this early commentary on sexism in TV meant at the time. Girls screamed all day long at school. Whether they saw a spider, or something disgusting in one of our workbooks, even when one of the boys ran into the girls changing rooms to make them jump during PE. So this was not irrational behaviour in my view back then.

The rest of the experience passed like a blur but I do remember thinking that the Mara manifesting itself as a snake was well realised and very believable. I also loved the added gore when the Mara is finally defeated and vomits bright-green goo as it writhes in agony on the floor. The image of Tegan's face appearing in the open mouth of the Mara was also a moment that had me clenching. Yet, despite some disturbing imagery and a Part 3 that I've tended to fast forward through on future watches, I was completely sold on *Doctor Who* on the basis of this first viewing.

So, what did *Snakedance* teach me, apart from not to trust circus mirrors again for fear of a snake skull materialising on my head? It taught me to seek out further adventures between the Doctor and Tegan. I simply had to know if he could fully trust her again after the events of *Snakedance*.

I was left with the sense that this was a companion to be wary of, although that final scene when they are sitting together and she is terrified by her ordeal did quell my suspicion a little. It also taught me that, no matter how odd, hyperactive or stern the Doctor could be, he was always sticking up for the underdog.

To me, he was the champion of the outsiders who didn't quite fit in because, in his weird and wonderful world, the Doctor didn't quite fit in either. And yet, in a way, he absolutely did. I'd already decided that the Doctor was just like

James Bond. Both could have different faces, both were accompanied by beautiful women and both would right all the wrongs and fight for the good guys. The only difference was that I hadn't seen the Doctor use a gun. And, to this day, I can honestly say that I have never seen 007 regenerate into another actor!

Not long after, I took the video to my cousin, Luke's, house in Harlow, Essex. I'd been telling him how brilliant *Doctor Who* was but he was unconvinced. He was more into Liverpool Football Club, WWF wrestling and his brand-new PlayStation. He was a few months older than me, and, although we shared similar interests, he wasn't into science-fiction, to put it mildly, and *Doctor Who* in particular.

Apart from *Star Trek: The Next Generation*, the brilliantly funny *Red Dwarf* and the short-lived *Space Precinct*, the tail end of Generation X that Luke and I belonged to didn't really have any outlet for intergalactic adventures. Especially those involving a centuries-old alien who could change his face. However, as I had been converted into a sci-fi fan in such a short space of time, I was sure I could do the same to Luke.

So, we sat down in his front room and a magical thing happened as the tape started. It began to go dark outside. All of a sudden, there was another dimension to watching a *Doctor Who* story. In the light, no evil can get you but, in the dark, the shadows are all around…

The psychological threat of the Mara became more menacing, the skull now seemed that little bit more malevolent and, even though Luke laughed at the sight of Tegan's head popping out of the mouth of the enlarged snake, it was still utterly chilling. By the end, I knew I hadn't snared him as I'd intended, but at least I'd broadened his televisual horizons. I'd also planted a vivid memory in his head that he still remembers 20 years later.

I still wanted someone to share this new found obsession, a yearning to sit down, get a bowl of salt and vinegar crisps and watch lots of stories with a friend who was just as engrossed as me. I may have failed with Luke but I had another four cousins I could try out!

Around this time, my Mum asked me who my favourite Doctor was. It was a close call, especially as I had only really seen two-and-a-bit incarnations of the Time lord from Gallifrey. I had to say Peter Davison as *Snakedance* was four episodes compared to *The TV Movie*'s one so it felt like I'd seen him more.

'Who's your favourite, Mum?' I asked.

'When I was little, Jon Pertwee was the one I remember watching with your uncle. He watched it right from the start. He was always hiding behind the sofa, especially when the Daleks came on!'

'I haven't seen the Daleks yet,' I told her. 'Are they really scary?'

'He thought they were!' she quipped. It would still be quite a long time until I would have my first meeting with the Daleks.

As I continued to wear out my one and only *Doctor Who* tape, Christmas drew nearer. I was dreaming up all kinds of *Who*-paraphernalia that I could ask Father Christmas for. And, of course, the biggest thing I wanted was more *Doctor Who* on VHS. But, before I put my special letter in the fireplace for Old Saint Nick to pick up, my dad called me downstairs.

I remember it being a cold, early November night but I could hear his voice bleeding through the floorboards and up into my room. I threw off my bed sheets and ran downstairs as fast as my little legs would carry me.

After racing into the living room, he showed me what he was watching. It was a programme called *BBC at 60* and it looked like an awards event, a bit like the Oscars that I'd seen on the news. Why did he want to show me this? All of a sudden, the words '*Doctor Who*' were mentioned.

I sat cross-legged on the floor mere inches from the TV screen and witnessed for the very first time a montage of all the Doctor's regenerations.

I caught a fleeting glimpse of a very old and grainy film clip of William Hartnell in a funny hat, asking the question '*Doctor Who?*'

I then remember seeing a dark and defiant Patrick Troughton scream 'You can't just change what I look like without consulting me!' although, at the time, I thought what he actually said was 'You cannot change the laws of physics!' I think a repeat of an original series episode of *Star Trek* may have lodged itself in my memory.

Suddenly, I witnessed the Doctor change - over and over again. I saw Jon Pertwee tumble out of the TARDIS doors and dissolve into Tom Baker. I then saw a ghostly Fourth Doctor melt into the Doctor I was growing to love, Peter Davison. This was followed by a colourful blur of faces that blew away into the Sixth, whose Art Garfunkel hair stood out as he shot up on screen.

There was then a confusing clip of what looked like a man-bat turning the Doctor over and his face was so blurred it resembled the outcome of my ice cream that I tended to play with until it was a gloopy mess at meal times. As memory serves, I then saw the Seventh's demise and the birth of the Eighth Doctor. I was mesmerised.

These images would be doodled in my school notebooks for the next few weeks. They burned into my brain so vividly that it was hard to get them out. Each regeneration, just like each of the Doctors, was so different to the one that preceded or followed. After the montage, Noel Edmonds (whose *House Party* show was perfect Saturday night viewing for me in the 1990s) announced that

Doctor Who had won the award for Most Popular Drama.

As I leant in closer still, two men in dinner suits stood up from the crowd and, amidst rapturous applause, proceeded to collect a gold statue. I thought it might be a Gotcha! (Authors Note: A Gotcha was a statuette presented to a well-known celebrity of the time who had been the subject of a cruel prank on *House Party* - think *Punk'd* on a BBC budget, kids of today!)

These two men were Peter Davison and Sylvester McCoy, two Doctors I didn't instantly recognise. They looked so different. But neither of them were the Doctor that long ago, were they? I remember working out on a calculator that *Snakedance* was shown just 13 years ago. Yes, it was almost double my age but I didn't think that the Fifth Doctor was nearly bald or that the Seventh wore glasses. Ah, the naivety of youth!

Luckily, my dad had been recording the programme so, for weeks after, I would dig out the tape and memorise how every-single regeneration looked. I was disappointed that I couldn't see what happened to the First and Second Doctors' demise but I had always been told that good things came to those who wait, no matter how impatient I was as a boy.

I asked Mum to keep an eye out for *Doctor Who* related bits and bobs on TV in case anything came up while I was at school. I was incredibly nervous that I might miss out on any tiny appearance of the Doctor. Most of the time, she caught various segments but I'll get back to that.

Then the most magical day in a child's life arrived. It was Christmas Day 1996 and, as always, my little sister and I eagerly tore into our presents at the crack of dawn, or even before because it was still dark. Unfortunately, I wasn't welcomed by many *Doctor Who* items but what I did get is still the only Christmas present I remember receiving that year.

This time, the front cover showed a Doctor in a long, multi-coloured scarf and it looked like he was being tied up by two men in white space helmets. The smaller picture in the corner of the cover was of a girl with no face, just a skeleton of metal and wires and two haunting eyes boggling out at me.

It was *The Android Invasion* and it was to serve as another important milestone in my early love for the series. For the first time, I was going to see the fabled Tom Baker in action.

Unfortunately for me though, my parents had other ideas. I wasn't allowed to watch it as we had guests coming to stay with us that day. It was Nan and Grandad again.

There were lots of toys to play with. Plus, as was tradition in my family, we would all sit around and watch the Disney film that ITV had selected to show that year (if memory serves me correctly, it was *Alice in Wonderland*).

The only time I did throw a bit of a tantrum that day was when I wasn't allowed to stay up and watch that year's *Only Fools and Horses Christmas Special*. Although I hadn't a clue as to what was going on, I was trying to laugh over the top of my father's demands to go to bed. In my defence, I did think that seeing Del Boy and Rodney as old men was downright hilarious.

I remember struggling to sleep and I can still remember hearing an eruption of laughter downstairs. It turns out now that this was the adult contingent of the Gribble family's reaction to the Trotters running through the streets as Batman and Robin. Had I known that Batman and Robin were making an appearance in *OFAH*, I think I'd have sat on the stairs, peeping through the banisters in the vain hope of glimpsing the television.

Sad and upset that I was too little to get involved in the merriment downstairs, I looked over at my pile of presents and picked out my *Doctor Who* video. Hurriedly yet as quiet as a mouse, I got out of bed and knelt by the pile, hugging the cassette to my chest. Tomorrow was going to be a good day, not just for all the leftover turkey but because I'd get to watch *The Android Invasion*. Whoever the Androids were or why they were invading.

'*Doctor Who*,' I thought to myself. 'No wonder there's a question in the title. All I ever do is ask questions about the silly programme!'

Frustrating though it was, my wait was rewarded and, on Boxing Day, after seeing the recording of *OFAH*, I had my first glimpse of the Fourth Doctor and his lovely assistant, Sarah Jane Smith. I think I loved *The Android Invasion* even more than *Snakedance*.

There was a deep connection between the Doctor and Sarah and I thought they must have gone way back. Maybe this girl was the Doctor's best friend.

Yet another title sequence, so crisp and hypnotic that it was an instant favourite. I remember thinking that the time vortex (whatever the word 'vortex' meant to me back then) had an aquatic quality. And the music was the best and most exciting interpretation yet, as was this "new" Doctor.

Tom Baker amazed me. He had a gravitas the others I had seen lacked and his strange, booming voice poured out of the television speaker like audible gold.

His floppy hat, that curly hair, the big and expressive eyes that seemed to scream an otherworldly existence. This guy really was from another planet.

I was unnerved by the finger guns that the Androids possessed and the fact that the Doctor and Sarah seemed to be friendly with these UNIT people (whoever they were). I also felt a tiny shard of fright when the Devesham village folk arrived on the back of a truck and were unloaded like cattle. I wondered if that's how my neighbours moved in!

By the end of the story, my desire for more *Doctor Who* was slowly gathering pace. But what was 1997 going to bring? More videos I hoped! Perhaps the people who made *The TV Movie* would change their minds and I would be able to get another look at Paul McGann's Byronesque incarnation.

As the credits rolled at the end of *The Android Invasion*, it was confirmed. *Doctor Who* was my new favourite show. And my quest had only just started!

CHAPTER THREE
SILENCE IN THE LIBRARY

Now that I think about it, *Doctor Who* was probably always there in my life – hidden in plain sight. And now that I had borne witness to a couple of stories from far back in the mists of time, I was starting to notice the show's presence more in everyday life. Ever since the broadcast of *The TV Movie*, I'd been frustrated by the lack of *Who* for me to watch, but the good Doctor had begun to pop up all over the place.

There were his weekly adventures in the all-too-brief *Radio Times* comic strips. He was also beginning to materialise on television more, albeit in very nostalgic and sometimes mick-taking skits on other people's shows. I remember a Clive James programme in which the Australian broadcaster had Anneke Wills, Nicola Bryant and Sophie Aldred sitting in the crowd, recalling moments in which sets wobbled and monsters were made of rubber and laughing along to how much screaming the former two were required to do. To my young mind, it didn't improve the show's image.

It felt like these people were retrospectively poking a stick sharply into the side of a wounded animal.

But there was one place where I could find the Doctor and didn't have to feel the heat of embarrassment on my face just as I felt when I saw a National Lottery programme laughing at the Monoids and almost gratuitously hinting at how rubbish they were.

It was a haven from the outside world that I could bask in. You see, all it took was a trip to the library…

Ever since I was small, I'd been enchanted by the sheer power a book possesses. It can take you out of your time and space (much like the TARDIS) and fill your mind with characters, worlds and stories only an individual can create in a completely unique way.

Unless you're reading a novelisation of a well-known TV show or film or a continuing series of books where the characters and their surroundings have already been visualised for you, you can pretty much start from scratch with a book. I used to piece together these worlds myself, constructing the looks and idiosyncrasies of the characters.

It's one of the reasons I used to write my own stories, though these would usually consist of two A4 pieces of paper folded in half and the plot would normally involve myself and my friends taking on a giant or an army of mummies in the vein of a *Scooby Doo* special.

If my head wasn't buried in a book or comic, I was normally thinking up these stories and playing them out in my head in a bid to while away the hours at school – especially when we were doing Maths which I have always struggled with on account of my dyscalculia.

So, imagine my delight when I bounced like Tigger into Haverhill library to flick through the Science Fiction shelf and came across a row of books with the *Doctor Who* logo emblazoned across their spines. My mouth fell open, wide enough to park a Dalek saucer. I'd never known that they made *Doctor Who* books too!

My mind filled with the ecstatic possibility of taking everything off the shelf, smuggling these paperbacks home and reading them back to back. I wanted to delve within the pages, live among the words and finally surface when the final page had been turned.

'Mum, Mum, look at this!' I implored as she made for the children's corner to find something to distract my fidgeting sister. By now, I think my parents' patience with my obsession was starting to wear thin but she indulged my excitement for a moment.

'Hmm…the only trouble is that these are adult books,' she said, flicking through the pages. 'You see? No pictures.'

I pulled myself up onto my tip toes to glance inside the book she'd picked from the shelf. She was right. No drawings of the Doctor and his friends, just words.

'That's okay, I know what the Doctor looks like. Please can I take them out?' I entreated.

Despite being convinced that these books were not suitable for this soon-to-be eight-year-old, she finally relented. I was allowed to take two home.

Giddy with joy, I started to pull each book off the shelf as it creaked under the stress of an overeager boy clawing away at its contents. I wanted to find out which books featured which Doctor. Some were easy to work out. I saw the face of the Seventh Doctor peering out at me from the cover of *Illegal Alien*. 'I'll have that one,' I declared as I put it on the floor.

I remember picking up a copy of Mark Gatiss' novel *The Roundheads* and declining it because the Second Doctor looked in a grumpy mood as he played on his recorder. In the end I settled for a book called *Vampire Science* purely based on the fact that I liked the title.

I resisted temptation to make a start on either of these novels until I got home. Besides, the library had that week's edition of *The Beano* in stock and I just had to have a peer into the hi jinx adventures of Dennis the Menace, Minnie the Minx, Billy Whizz and of course, The Bash Street Kids. Especially as, for some reason, I wasn't allowed to get *The Beano* that week.

What I remember of reading *Vampire Science* was a feeling of frustration and anti-climax. Not long into the Doctor and his new companion Sam's battle with interplanetary vampires who fought the Time Lords long ago, it gradually dawned on me that these were strangers to me. I really struggled to get into the story.

I really found it hard to maintain concentration on such a complex novella and came to realise that, if this was the only way I could indulge in any more Eighth Doctor adventures (especially as *The TV Movie* looked like it was going to be a mere flash in the pan), then maybe the latest incarnation wasn't for me.

I needed something visual, something to relate to, which I really couldn't with Sam because I didn't know what she looked like or what made her tick and it was tough for someone so young to look for these little character-forming traits. It went against my usual ability to use my imagination to depict a new person in fiction form, but on this occasion I really struggled. So, my window in the world of *Doctor Who,* through the companion, was flawed. And, as she was a new assistant herself, the Doctor didn't know her that well either. In the words of the great Tom Baker at a convention, looking around at his predecessors and successors 'Who are these people?'

What I really needed to do was to get to know these other Doctors better before tackling their tales in paperback form. But how was I ever going to watch them? With no money and just a couple of VHS copies of old stories to watch in the meantime, I had no idea how to visit these vintage adventures. But, as if my magic, that same library in Haverhill was to hold the answer to my prayers.

In the oft-visited video section, I'd started to notice that more and more *Doctor Who* tapes were gathering on the shelf. Looking back now, it seems entirely feasible that a local fan had possibly conducted a clear-out or even moved from the area altogether and decided to donate their tapes. Indeed, this was not the only BBC Science Fiction show to suddenly appear in what was becoming my favourite library in the universe.

From out of the unknown, there were also video copies of *The Hitchhikers Guide to the Galaxy,* which was soon to suck me into its total perspective vortex of magnificence, and *Blake's 7* (which I shall come back to later) but, of course, those battered, dirty-looking *Doctor Who* tapes took my full attention.

The one that drew my attention most was a dark purple spine that said *The Troughton Years*. As I inspected the front cover, I was taken aback by the black and white face of Patrick Troughton. For a split second, my mind told me that it wasn't a picture of the Doctor's second incarnation. It was my Gramps staring back at me. I'd never spotted it before but that mop of jet black hair, the chin, those remarkable eyes. If it hadn't been for the white-speckled beard that Gramps wore on his pointed chin, then he would have been the spitting image! At that point, I decided to take this video home and watch it as much as I could, over and over again.

Again my mum warned me. She told me that his stuff was in black and white and that it even said so on the back of the video cover. I told her I didn't care. I wanted to see *Doctor Who* before it changed over to colour.

The only thing I'd ever seen in black and white were Laurel and Hardy films and early Saturday morning repeats of *The Munsters*. Reluctantly, again, my mum paid up the rental price and I just couldn't wait to go home and watch what to me was rare, vintage *Doctor Who*.

To find a tape like this was like finding gold dust on the moon. I was about to open yet another chapter in my burgeoning fandom…I was going to watch not just any old *Doctor Who* but *Doctor Who* that was thirty years old, the kind that my dad remembered watching. He'd already told me that he could recall seeing a line of never ending Daleks on a conveyor belt, Cybermen tearing their way out of cocoons in the ice, Yeti in the underground and a terrifying Emperor Dalek looming large over the Doctor and his friends as his voice boomed out of the speakers and into the nightmares of the children of the 1960s.

CHILD OUT OF TIME

Finally, I was going to get a glimpse into the episodes he had seen when he was my age. Sadly, however, as it was Easter and he was at work, it meant I was going to have to watch the tape alone. I don't think that I had read the cover blurb though. I thought that *The Troughton Years* was going to be a greatest hits of the Second Doctor's era.

Sadly, it wasn't. Following a version of the *Doctor Who* theme that sounded like a terrible rehash of a bad disco track (almost the kind that would pollute the air at a school party), the familiar face of Jon Pertwee materialised in a snowy puddle outside the BBC's long-lost Lime Grove Studios. I was over the moon when he introduced the very first regeneration scene. As the image of the First Doctor blurred and changed to the Second, I wondered what on Earth Pertwee meant by that sequence being the "only remaining material" from that story, *The Tenth Planet*.

He repeated the phrase again when stood next to a rather mangy looking Yeti costume as he introduced the only remaining episode of *The Abominable Snowmen*. I must confess that, by this point, I was rather disappointed by what I was watching. Had I made the right choice of tape to rent out? Should I have gone for the double video lying next to it on that shelf? The one that said, *The Sontaran Experiment* and *Genesis of the Daleks* on the spine? Maybe that one would have been much better than the first few minutes of this tape which had me reaching for the remote control to turn it off.

Then, all of a sudden, the screen bled from colour to black and white and the monochrome swirls ebbed and swelled on the monitor. This new incarnation of the theme music was like nothing I'd heard before and so much better than the two I had. Probably because it was longer.

It might have been the two-tone imagery and the haunting face of Patrick Troughton that loomed towards me but, for the first time, *Doctor Who* felt creepy.

What happened next was enough to catapult my adrenaline levels sky high. The picture cut to a couple of youngsters cornered in a cave by a Yeti, its blood curdling roar shaking the TV and flooding my room with fear. At this point, my little sister had turned away and gone back to playing with her dolls. It was clearly already too much for her. I watched on and saw a kilted young man hitting a support away from its hoardings and crushing the attacking abominable snowman under what looked and sounded like large polystyrene blocks.

I had no idea what had led to this couple (Who were named Jamie and Victoria) running for their lives from this great hairy beastie. There was no hint as to what the plot was, where the Doctor and his friends were and what on Earth was going on in general. But, in just a minute and a half of Episode 2, I was hooked. It didn't take long for me to develop a platonic love for Patrick Troughton's interpretation of the Time Lord. Much like Peter Davison's performance in *Snakedance*, he encapsulated everything I imagined the Doctor could be and more. He was like a cheeky uncle. I felt safe watching him and, although he didn't look as tall or strong as the other versions of the Doctor I'd already seen, he was definitely the same character as all of them. In fact, they all seemed a little similar to him in their demeanour.

To me, the monochrome images that flickered and jumped on that square television in our living room took me out of my home and into a dark and mysterious world where the shadows seemed to come to life and the voices appeared to echo at every syllable uttered and every sound effect that bounced off the walls of the dank and forbidding monastery.

This lone episode of what later transpired to be a lost classic was enough to capture the imagination of not just me, but for the first time, my friends too. Soon after what must have been my fifth renting of the tape, came my birthday and I was allowed to invite a few friends over for dinner, cake and games.

As the celebrations progressed, I wanted to try to convince my friends that this show I'd been talking about, this *Doctor Who* fellow in his magical blue box, was not some fevered imagining. It was real and, what's more, it was cool. To drive this point home, I decided that the best thing to do was to make them watch Episode 2 of *The Abominable Snowmen* and decide for themselves just how awesome it was.

Again, just like my mother, there were a few grumbles regarding the episode's black and white status. There seemed to be a slight prejudice back then regarding shows that were not blessed with cutting edge CGI effects or filmed in everyday technicolour. But as I explained to them, black and white was cool, it was different and it made what they were about to watch exciting on a level that even *Thunderbirds* couldn't provide.

Okay, so that last statement may have been a fib at the time, but I was desperate to find friends who would fall in love with this show just as I had done. I'd failed to convince my cousin, Luke, that *Doctor Who* was great. Would I be able to convince my nearest and dearest friends?

For the next twenty-five minutes, all four of them sat on the carpet, transfixed by the flickering magic that I had bestowed upon them. Not a word was uttered. Even my mother recollects how silent we all were. It was an incredible moment. Five young boys, rendered motionless by the sheer brilliance of a thirty-year-old grainy, damaged copy of a long-lost story from an almost forgotten programme.

CHILD OUT OF TIME

Looking back now, it was a miracle that the print (among many more as I was to learn) even existed and was even watchable in that state. Now I know that this video was released long before the days of the Doctor Who Restoration Team and their Vidfire machine that made old Sixties classics look spotless again.

We didn't even notice the hole in the soundtrack when the Monks are singing and the action cuts to the Doctor and his friends inspecting the silver control sphere. Although it did seem a bit random that the dialogue started with the word "Victoria". But back then, it looked so different to the TV shows that my friends and I were used to watching.

That made *Doctor Who* unique and was one of the reasons why I had become obsessed with it.

On my first viewing of the tape, I'd been utterly confused by Jon Pertwee's presence and his saying that 'the archive was cut back...and Pat's era was affected most.' What did he mean? Had they destroyed episodes? Surely not! I dismissed this and continued with Episode 3 of *The Enemy of the World*, which was instantly great for having two Patrick Troughtons in it, and terrible for pretty much everything else. It was a snore fest. Barely anything happened. Apart from a couple of funny lines from a jaded yet highly entertaining Aussie chef in a kitchen that Victoria was now working in, I didn't find much in the episode to earn my attention.

However, it was remarkable just how comfortable I felt watching this TARDIS team of the Second Doctor, Jamie and Victoria. After just two episodes, I truly believed in them. They seemed like a lot of fun and, in Jamie, who became my first male companion, I had someone to look up to like an older brother. He behaved like a true hero, putting Yeti to the sword (literally), and protecting the Doctor (for whom he clearly had great affection) and Victoria (for whom he clearly had a crush).

I didn't know when or where these two came from (well, Scotland, naturally for Jamie!) but I didn't care. This was my favourite TARDIS team.

As the tape continued, I was surprised to discover that, although Troughton's run was made in black and white, he had appeared in the show in colour and alongside other Doctors I hadn't even seen yet! The clip with the Brigadier (whose name I'd heard in *The Android Invasion* and whose image I'd seen in that *Radio Times* pull-out) really amused me as the Doctor and his old friend were cornered in a cave by a Yeti. When the Doctor rummaged through his pockets and discovered only an apple core, some sweets and a sling shot, that confirmed it for me.

Patrick Troughton, the man who had kept the show going after Hartnell left, the man who had died two years before I was born, was MY Doctor.

CHILD OUT OF TIME

To finish the tape, Jon Pertwee introduced something called *The Space Pirates* which, to an eight-year-old boy, is probably one of the most exciting titles for anything you could hear. Pirates! In SPACE! What a shame that the quality didn't live up to the billing as I found the episode a boring, tedious opera among the stars. And I hated opera back then. Every time there was one on the television, especially over Christmas, I'd retire to my room and either play with my *Captain Scarlet* toys or read a well-worn issue of *The Beano*. I quickly learned to fast forward through the scenes with Milo Clancey and Major Ian Warne and the woman with the stupid hair/hat.

I just wanted to see the Doctor, Jamie and... wait, who's this Zoe? Where's Victoria. I wasn't too sure I liked Zoe on this first meeting. She didn't seem to possess a cool head like the Doctor and Jamie. I was profoundly shocked when Clancey burst in at the end and shot the young Scot. I was sure he was dead. No! How could they? And then I was even more disappointed when the third episode wasn't shown straight after, the events of the story being explained by a not-so-helpful Jon Pertwee.

Despite my love for *The Troughton Years* tape, I was so confused by the lack of information on what happened in the other parts to these three, very random stories. And one question kept bugging me. Where were the other episodes?

It seemed like no time at all since my last visit to the library and, after my disappointment at what was to offer on the literary end of the *Doctor Who* range, I was growing frustrated. I'd only seen three-and-a-bit stories, attempted to read two novels (and struggled with both) and discovered a Doctor I loved but whose episodes were sporadic for some mysterious reason. What I needed was two things. Another FULL story to reignite my fire and a book explaining some more of the folklore of *Doctor Who* to help plug the glaring gaps in my knowledge.

I searched the non-fiction, TV tie-in section of the library and found a book with its cover facing out to the browsing public. On the front were two faces, both so familiar to me now but also strangers to me at the same time. Like people you meet at a party then see again but don't remember their names. Only I did know this duo. It was Jon Pertwee and Tom Baker and this book was called DOCTOR WHO – THE SEVENTIES – BY DAVID J HOWE, MARK STAMMERS AND STEPHEN JAMES WALKER. I grabbed it from its place on the shelf, rummaged in my pocket to find my library card and rented it out without even asking my mum's permission. In my haste, it hadn't occurred to me that this was the first book I had got out by myself. And what a book it was!

As a boy, I had an unquenchable thirst for facts and knowledge. So, a long-running and intriguing programme like *Doctor Who* was perfect for me. I can vividly remember lying on my bedroom floor, my feet up on the radiator (which I was never allowed to do as my parents feared me kicking it off the wall), meticulously investigating the two Doctors who were featured, their companions, their enemies and the episode titles. From the pictures within, I came to the conclusion that Mary Tamm's Romana was absolutely gorgeous, as was Louise Jameson's Leela, though that was probably because it looked like she didn't wear many clothes.

I pored over every screen grab of action from the stories and decided that I really wanted to see those that had the most ambiguous titles. *Spearhead from Space*, *Inferno*, *Frontier in Space*, *The Seeds of Doom* and *The Talons of Weng-Chiang* were but a few that grabbed my attention. I had to look out for them in my library. It was my only chance to see more episodes.

Moreover, this treasure trove of facts was yet another glimpse through the looking glass at what was clearly a golden age of the show. My mind was furnished with a broader understanding of *Doctor Who*. From what I read, the Seventies also looked pretty good!

To compound my education of the Seventies and my new found love for the Troughton years, I became the lucky recipient of yet another video in the meantime. This one was the 1973 Jon Pertwee classic, *The Green Death*. It was another gift, this time a late birthday one from my Nan on my mother's side. Considering that I'd recently read about it, the story more than lived up to my expectations. I instantly fell for the departing Jo Grant and really felt the Doctor's pain when she decided to stay in the Nut Hutch with Professor Clifford Jones. Although it was my first Pertwee adventure, I could feel the pathos and emotions that were as broad on-screen as a giant maggot was long, which looked equally gruesome and cool at the same time.

I loved the inclusion of UNIT and the presence of Brigadier Lethbridge Stewart, played by the brilliant Nicholas Courtney, who made me sit to attention as though he was in the room. And now that I'd met him properly, I could tell why he was such a good friend to the Doctor and had popped up so frequently in the magazine and clips that I'd seen.

Their relationship seemed to be built on mutual respect and a bit of friction in the clash of characters. As for the villains of the piece, mainly the omnipresent BOSS and his brainwashed employees at Global Chemicals, they were highly threatening and, considering the only monsters of the story were a by-product of the waste the company was literally keeping underground. The sinister human element captivated me.

The Third Doctor was a colossus in the story. In many ways, *The Green Death* is perhaps Pertwee's best performance. He is hilarious when undercover as the Welsh milkman and the cleaning lady, strong and imposing when taking on Stevens's guards, charming and concerned by the ecological devastation that awaits them in the improbable-to-pronounce Welsh mining town of Llanfairfach. He even taught me what the word, 'serendipity' meant when analysing the feverish ramblings of Professor Jones after being bitten by a giant maggot!

I remember making notes in one of my old school books concerning *The Green Death*. Looking at my terrible, childish handwriting, I can see that the story's stark moralising theme had got through to me to such an extent that I felt compelled to send *Blue Peter* a drawing of Bonnie the dog putting litter in the bin, for which I received a green badge not long after. I'm not sure that's the desired effect that producer Barry Letts had in mind when writing the story with Robert Sloman, but it was a darn good drawing!

After declaring that *The Green Death* was my new favourite story, despite mostly ignoring Parts Two and Three after my first viewing and really picking up interest when the UNIT soldiers arrive at the start of Part Four, I skipped off to the library again and again and again in the hope of finding many more *Doctor Who* stories to indulge in.

However, soon after, the stock had begun to diminish, with only a couple of videos in at any given time and I began to wonder if I had a rival for the treasures of these well-watched and worn classic videos. Or perhaps a peer to share my love for a show which seemed so alive to me but long dead to the rest of the world. In the windy school playgrounds, I was all alone again in my love for *Doctor Who*…

CHAPTER FOUR
ESCAPE TO DANGER

There comes a time in every little boy's life when he loves something so much that he would do anything to have it. It could be a toy, sitting proudly on the shelf of some vast Toys 'R' Us warehouse somewhere in the Home Counties, tantalizingly out of reach of those stretching up on their tiptoes with their searching fingertips pointing to the heavens. Or it could be a sticker collection, for example the Panini Premier League stickers or Pokémon cards that spent much of the 1990s on the playground black market, with many a hopeless child exchanging his dinner money or homework duties just for a shiny Charizard.

For me though, my obsession led to something I had never done before or since. And I didn't have to haggle with my friends to trade my insane stash of Diglet and power-up cards just to get a Pikachu special. My determination for more *Doctor Who*, I'm ashamed and slightly proud to admit, involved my taking something out of my school library on, well, let's just say 'extended loan.'

It was a book. Not one of your Enid Blytons or Roald Dahls but a very special one that I'd been drawn to. It didn't look that appetizing to the eyes of your average schoolchild as it stood battered and torn by the winds of time and many grubby fingerprints adorned its dirty cream cover. Yet, despite its beaten state, it was one of the most special things I'd ever found and, considering it must have been in my school for decades, it had been under my nose the whole time.

It was a Target book. Not just any old Target book. It was a literary realisation of something called *Doctor Who and the Web of Fear*.

But, before I reveal more, I need to take you slightly further back in time to a visit to an old second hand book shop on the east coast of England...

I have always loved summertime. The bright blue skies, the warm blanket of sun that goes hand in hand with the refreshing cool breeze always takes me back to those endless summer holidays of the late 1990s.

Maybe my love for the season was also due in part to my birthday falling in June and, more often than not, it was half term week and I wasn't at school. Soon after a beautiful cake made by my Mum had been reduced to crumbs on a plate and my presents were put away neatly under my bed, the home stretch to the end of the school year would begin.

Another year at Steeple Bumpstead Primary had dissolved into the ether. Another year closer to being old enough to leave education altogether and start doing what I wanted in life. Another year closer to freedom.

One of the advantages of having grandparents who lived on the coast was that we took regular trips to the seaside. Despite not being a very strong swimmer (I had completed my 50m by then and was a dab hand at breast stroke but ended up resembling a drowning horse in a vat of treacle whenever I so much as attemped a front crawl), I could still find many things to do. Building sand castles, digging trenches, seeing how far I could throw stones whilst trying to avoid the sea of swimmers or losing myself in a comic or book.

I struggle to recall whether I'd mentioned my frustration at the lack of *Doctor Who* in my life but, if I hadn't, then my Grandad had cottoned on pretty quickly. He told me that he remembered seeing the very first episode way back on the 23rd of November 1963. He regaled me stories of how my dad and his brother had been captivated by the show, much like I was, and how they used to 'hide behind the sofa' whenever the Daleks, Cybermen and the Yeti burst onto their little TV monitor.

Grandad even told me that there used to be Dalek costumes that children could wear and that they could run around exterminating family members, friends or school teachers if they were in the vicinity. They even had Dalek figurines and annuals back in the day. This blew my mind. *Doctor Who* books, toys and costumes? I felt a twinge of self-pity as I realised I had none and curled into a sulking ball.

'You don't wanna do that! There's a bookshop up the road. I can ask the man who owns the place to keep a look out for you? Then, next time you come to visit, we can go along and see if they have any?'

'Good old Grandad,' I thought. He's on my side in my quest. I told him I'd love to and then promptly forgot about it as I seem to recall he put a James Bond film on to divert my attention away from the good Doctor for just a couple of hours. One of my rituals upon visiting that little bungalow on the corner of the street in Clacton was to indulge in my grandad's video collection. He had taped every James Bond film that had been shown to date onto video cassette (except *On Her Majesties Secret Service*, because he thought George Lazenby was more than inept as 007) and, in doing so, he created yet another addiction that I've carried into my adulthood.

For the next couple of weeks, I remember lying in bed at night dreaming about this Aladdin's Cave of vintage *Doctor Who* material. Even though I knew that it was just a bookshop, I harboured hope that maybe, just maybe, there might also be a Dalek costume in there too.

'Those Daleks,' I pondered. 'What are they?' At this point I still hadn't seen them in action. I knew they screamed 'EXTERMINATE!' every time they killed someone but, apart from that and the look, I had no clue as to how dangerous to the Doctor they were. What were their motives? Why did they hate the Doctor so much? I wished so hard that there was some Dalek paraphernalia in this already fabled bookshop just so that I could investigate them further.

It wasn't long until Grandad and I took the mile-long walk through the coastal sunshine to see what the bookshop had in store for me. The bungalow was situated at the bottom of a hill and, as a kid, I always saw the walk up the street to the peak as akin to taking on Mount Everest in flip-flops. Instead of wailing and complaining about the journey, I was always driven to take the hill on and win in my desire to see what this bookshop had in store for me.

When we eventually arrived, the shop was far from what I was expecting. It stood opposite a bookmakers that later transpired to be the one my grandad frequented at the weekends. I looked up at the banner that hung above the doorway. There, against a purple backdrop, was the word *Bookworm*. It looked small, too small to house the army of Daleks I was hoping to find within.

Upon entering the *Bookworm*, we were greeted by the shopkeeper. He was a nice man in his late thirties or early forties, whose most prominent feature was a sandy brown moustache. He was very welcoming and I was quick to cotton on to the fact that Grandad had already mentioned my rapidly growing need for *Doctor Who* books to this friendly gentleman. Gleefully, he directed the pair of us to an alleyway teeming with books of all shapes and sizes.

I was transfixed by the sheer variety of literature he had. I even noticed out of the corner of my eye some football books but I wouldn't be returning for them until my *Doctor Who* fascination had well and truly died down.

As we walked past shelf after shelf of wonder, I tripped a little on some small paperback books that had been left in a pile to the right of the book shelf. Grandad yelped at me to watch my step, possibly fearing the compensation bill if my clumsiness had damaged them! Kneeling down to straighten the pile, I noticed the emblem on the front cover of the topmost book.

It was a *Doctor Who* novel! I dived into the tottering tower of books which must have stood a foot high off the floor and squealed in delight when I realised that these were all *Doctor Who* novels! And they weren't original fiction like the ones I'd discovered in Haverhill library. These were titles I recognised as novelisations of the TV stories.

I hadn't yet mastered the knack of memorizing which story featured which Doctor, so there was a degree of guesswork accompanying the trawl through the covers that didn't carry an incarnation of the good Time Lord.

I could have sworn blind that *The Leisure Hive* was a Peter Davison story as the logo on the cover and the year it was published corresponded with the Fifth Doctor's era. I was also sure that *The Time Warrior* must be an adventure with Tom Baker at the helm as Sarah Jane Smith was mentioned in the browning pages that felt so crisp and ancient in my hands. The front cover to *The Enemy of the World* baffled me as there was no clue as to who the surly, bald man was or his attractive blonde assistant.

'How many can I have?' I asked Grandad.

He produced a shiny 50 pence piece from his pocket and handed it over to me. 50p!?

'That won't get me very much at all,' I said. My grandparents had a habit of not giving out much pocket money on our visits. The only comparison I could use was that a *Beano* comic cost 45p. And with these books being older than me, I didn't think I would stand a chance with even covering the cost of one.

As I remember, there were at least two dozen Target novelisations on that bookshop floor. I was petrified that I would end up going home with none. That couldn't happen, I thought to myself. This had been the biggest haul of *Doctor Who* goodies I'd ever come across. To leave the shop without at least some of these sought-after treasures under my arm would be a catastrophe.

I'd been kneeling in one position for far too long and had to peel my bare knees off the rough carpet that looked as old as the books. Fighting the pins and needles, I staggered over to the bookshop keeper and asked him how much the books were.

He had overheard my shock that my budget was a measly 50 pence and looked up at Grandad and declared 'He can have five for 50p, ten pence each.'

Jackpot!

With a smile longer than the Orient Express in space, I thanked him and hurled myself back at the floor and the pile of novellas. Five of these books would be mine. In my eagerness, I started to rummage away the books, being very careful not to damage any. But which five should I choose? I was determined to discard any that I'd already seen on video. Not that that narrowed down my choices!

In the end I plumped for *Doctor Who and the Cybermen*, *Tomb of the Cybermen*, *Image of the Fendahl*, *The Five Doctors* and *Earthshock*. I remember being puzzled as to why Peter Davison was on the front cover of the last one, brandishing what resembled a blaster.

I was already well aware of the rule that the Doctor would never use a gun to kill. I also thought that the blue, rectangular portrait of the first five Doctors in the foreground of *The Five*

Doctors novelisation was a sticker and tried pulling it off before thinking better of it.

After the transaction was completed, I walked back to the bungalow with more of a spring in my step. I couldn't wait to indulge in my new books. But now, for the first time in my life as a *Doctor Who* fan, I was spoiled for choice.

Since I'd developed a recent affinity for the Second Doctor, I decided that I needed more Troughton in my life, no matter how enticing *The Five Doctors* novelisation seemed. So, once we had got back and eaten lunch, I raced into the spare bedroom and hurled myself onto the bed. Nan hated me doing this, so I'd developed an intricate and genius way of leaping onto the mattress without making the bed squeak.

For the rest of that afternoon, I whiled away the hours lying upside down with my head off the foot of the bed reading *Doctor Who and the Cybermen* by Gerry Davis.

It was an atmospheric recounting of a story set on some kind of Moonbase that controlled the Earth's weather in what seemed like the distant future. As first encounters go, this was my first exposure to the deadly silver giants and, even in prose form, they were enthralling, cold to the eye of the beholder and a deadly threat to the base-under-siege.

I was unable to finish the book that afternoon as my parents usually left the coast early so that my little sister and I could settle back home easier after a long day. Most of the time, I would be lulled into a deep sleep by the slow rocking motion of my dad's red Vauxhall Cavalier and tempted into a slumber by the hot summer sun.

But this time, I fought back my midday weariness and soldiered on. I remember being impressed by the Doctor's two companions I had never met before, Ben and Polly. I loved the dynamic the duo had with the Doctor and Jamie – when the latter was fully conscious that is!

The blurb on the back of the paperback told just how deadly these Cybermen were. With plastic and steel to replace 'diseased' limbs, the strength of ten men and computers for brains, I could easily imagine that, one day, these men might be real.

And the icing on the cake for me was the rhetorical question of whether the Doctor could, 'defeat an enemy whose threat is almost as great as that of the mighty Daleks.'

That description alone confirmed the Cybermen as my favourite monsters, even though I had yet to see them on screen. But I was a little perplexed by the 'Polly cocktail'. I always knew that the Doctor and his friends would triumph at the end of the day but for such a powerful enemy as the Cybermen to be vanquished by something as simple as a concoction of fire extinguisher and nail varnish made them a little less intimidating. I wondered if that was how they were defeated all the time. How would that make them almost as powerful as the Daleks?

Still, the thought of the Earth's weather being controlled by a group of lunar weathermen in 2070 was very cool, I thought, and I liked the suspicious and authoritative Hobson who was the head honcho of the assembly. And the Doctor didn't seem as comedic or assuring as I had seen him in those orphaned episodes on *The Troughton Years*.

Maybe, the greater the enemy, the more serious his demeanour became. I wouldn't find out until I found the story on VHS.

The next novelisation I read was *The Five Doctors*. I took it to school in my blue carrying folder where it sat with my *Hercules* pencil case and school books with drawings of Tie Fighters and X-Wings doing battle scrawled everywhere. We used to have an hour a week allotted to quiet, independent reading, where a simple raised hand could summon our teacher for anybody struggling with the words or phrases.

I got about halfway through the novel, written by a man called Terrance Dicks who I was already beginning to like as an author, and needed a little assistance from my teacher.

She was far from my favourite. She was around 60 years of age and as fastidious and unpleasant as an overly disciplinary soldier. She could have been a Sergeant-Major and I was always amazed at those in my year who were not reduced to gibbering wrecks in the face of her short temper and shouting fits. In the space of that year, she had reduced me to tears more than anyone else has before or since. But it wasn't all bad in her class. I won the Best Christmas Cake competition after all!

For reasons of fairness, I shall not use her name here, but said teacher used to shout some of my classmates into submission on a regular basis. She was as old school as they came and was more terrifying to this eight-year-old than any Cybermen or *Doctor Who* monster could be. Because, at the end of the day, they were just figments of brilliantly twisted imaginations, but my teacher was real.

I had plucked the courage up from somewhere within me to put my hand up and ask for her help. She got up from her seat behind her unusually tidy desk and glided towards me.

'Yes, Hayden?' she whispered. Her face wore a quizzical expression. I was proud to be amongst one of the best in my class when it came to English language and literature.

I gulped hard. 'Miss, what's this word?'

'Do you mean, how should I pronounce it?'

'Yes, Miss.'

She bent lower to my level and peered at the pages. She then looked at me with bewilderment and mouthed the letters to me.

'R-A-S-T-O-N.'

I tore my gaze away from her thin lips and mouthed the letters to myself. Then, after a few seconds of silence, I exclaimed:

'OH IT'S PRONOUNCED RASTON. IT'S A RASTON WARRIOR ROBOT!'

My teacher's eyes turned to wildfire and she spat at me to be silent. What my friends must have thought of my sudden outburst, I'll never know. But at least I now knew how to say 'Raston.' I think possibly I was looking for a little bit of attention as the word 'Raston' isn't the most difficult word in the world. Or any world, for that matter.

Even if it did nothing but leave my teacher pouring scorn on me as she retreated back to her old fashioned desk, I had coaxed a chuckle from some of my classmates.

I sometimes did this to attract welcome attention from the girls in my class. Somehow behaving in an abstract and non-conformist way even at our young age seemed to make them like me. Maybe it's a technique I should use more often. I wonder how many numbers I would get from single women today if I stood in Cambridge Market Square and bellowed 'REVERSE THE POLARITY OF THE NEUTRON FLOW!' at the top of my voice?

To me, *The Five Doctors* was almost a Greatest Hits of *Doctor Who*. It seemed to assemble everything that had been great and good about the show up until that point and every

Doctor was included. I remember trying to visualise William Hartnell and Peter Davison arguing about the best way to make it to Rassilon's Tower. I also tried to form a picture of what the Master looked like and settled on the Roger Delgado guise (as this was still the only face I'd seen of the Doctor's arch enemy). And, more importantly, the novel allowed me a glimpse into the Doctor's home planet, Gallifrey, for the very first time.

Despite a fleeting mention in *The TV Movie* and a delicious account of what the night sky looked like on that planet, I'd not yet been privy to what the planet of the Time Lords really was like. To be perfectly honest, it made this mythical, almost untouchable race seem nothing more than pompous politicians. Even in prose form, the Time Lords were just as treacherous and conniving as those in the Government seemed to be to my parents.

But a passage that really grabbed my attention was the revelation that the Doctor had visited Cambridge. For once, the TARDIS hadn't materialised on a faraway alien planet but had landed quite literally on my doorstep! To read that the Fourth Doctor took his companion Romana (whoever she was) punting behind Kings College before being taken out of time by the baddie of this story sent me reeling.

Here I was trying to find any outlet of *Doctor Who* that it was possible to encounter and the

CHILD OUT OF TIME

Time Lord had been in my neck of the woods all along! And yet, it made me wonder.

How come I'd never heard of this before? Why wasn't there a notice at the tourist information centre near Drummer Street announcing that *Doctor Who* had once filmed here? I wondered if this was just a segment of the book that had been made up and was not included in its TV version.

Or, if it had been filmed, was this sequence ever broadcast? It must have been, I thought, and I made a note in my ideas book to seek this story out. There was no clue as to what the episode was called, so I was resigned to just hoping that a Cambridge landmark was included on the front cover of the VHS.

Once again, however, it was the Second Doctor who stole the show, forming an instantly likable partnership with Brigadier Lethbridge-Stewart. From the clip I'd seen on *The Troughton Years* tape, I instantly knew the relationship they shared was one of respect, loyalty and of course a collective experience of fighting alien monsters.

This sudden influx of Target books led to further trips to that *Bookworm* shop on the Kings Avenue. Month after month, my collection of *Doctor Who* stories grew. From *The Sea Devils* to *The Visitation*, I managed to build a collection of past adventures from the first five Doctors. Oddly enough, I never came across any novelisations from the Sixth and Seventh Doctors but their time would come.

As I still lacked the money to buy the videos and see these stories, the books were the best outlet I could find. Here, my imagination could wander, finding a structure to the locations and characters and building them around the familiarity of whatever incarnation of the Doctor was the protagonist and the companions and villains I had seen pictures of. It was so easy to do now that I had seen a little more of the show and no longer endured the struggles I'd encountered when trying to read one of the Eighth Doctor's novels. And it was through these books that I felt more connected to the past than ever before.

I remember sitting in my garden, recognising that what I was doing was exactly what my parents' generation had done when wanting to visit the *Doctor Who* stories of way back when. This must have been what it was like before videos were invented.

But there were still gaps in my fandom. And one of them was a yawning chasm where the Doctor's most fearful enemy should have been.

Later on in the year, I achieved a major coup by finding and purchasing three Dalek stories - *The Dalek Invasion of Earth*, *The Power of the Daleks* and *The Day of the Daleks* . Finally, it was time to experience what I found to be metal pepper pots first hand. Like many other things intended to send children scuttling behind the sofa or hiding behind a cushion, the Daleks were supposed to strike terror wherever they trundled.

However, I was never afraid of the Daleks. Maybe if I'd seen them before I read about them, then the story might have been different. From the images I had seen, the design of the monster was beyond cool. I had no idea that there was a creature inside until I read *Power* which, of course, was Troughton's debut story and so depicted a very graphic rendition of the regeneration.

As I'd already read about Ben and Polly, I was delighted to find out that they were the first companions to witness a change of one Doctor to another. But no matter how hard I tried, I couldn't finish the book. It wasn't that the text was hard to follow. Indeed, I found the author John Peel to be a vivid and descriptive guide throughout proceedings, but I wanted to maintain a degree of mystery regarding the story. That also went for the other two Dalek tales. The creatures had such a legend woven throughout the fabric of the show and anything I read would be a spoiler. So, from here on in, I kept those books on the shelf in my bedroom and waited until I could see all three on video.

My self-discipline would remain resolute until one day in my school library. Despite my obsession with writing and literature, I didn't frequent that small room in my school. I can still picture it now though. It was a multi-coloured haven for readers of all ages (well, ages 4 to 11) and, from time to time, if a pupil had forgotten their reading book, then they would be asked to go to the library and pick one out to read for that afternoon and return afterwards.

On this day, I had left my book at home. It would have been so easy to get my teacher to ring home and ask my mum to drop it off as we only lived across the street from Steeple Bumpstead Primary School.

But, as I knew that I'd already risked the untethered wrath of my teacher, who when angry used to pull a face like Terrence Hardiman in *The Demon Headmaster* when miffed, I decided to ask whether I could take a book out instead. Luckily, she must have been in a good mood that day as I was allowed to venture into the library alone.

As I ran my finger along the spines of the various books on offer, I came across a thin, crumbling book. It attracted my attention more than the many RL Stine's *Goosebumps* novels that lined the shelf.

As the title was written down the spine, I turned my head on its side and read out loud the text.

'*Doctor Who…and…THE WEB OF FEAR!*'

I was shocked and excited beyond belief. I couldn't believe that there was a *Doctor Who* book in my school library. As I tore it away from its place sandwiched between those *Goosebumps* books, I was filled with excitement when I saw that it was a Patrick Troughton story.

There he was on the front, looming large over what looked like an Abominable Snowmen and a soldier brandishing his gun ready to attack.

I hurried back to my classroom and tripped up on a bag strap that was poking out of the cloakroom ready to entangle me. I picked myself up, wriggled out of the loop and quickly settled back into my chair and began reading. All of time stopped around me. From the very first chapter, thrillingly called Return of Evil, I was immersed in the story.

I was there when Professor Travers (who I already knew from that lone episode of *The Abominable Snowmen*) was demanding his inactive Yeti back from the stubborn Emil Julius. I was standing in the TARDIS while the Doctor and Jamie bickered over whether the dematerialising light was flashing or not. I stepped from the Police Box into a deserted London Underground and along with a familiar yet younger version of Lethbridge-Stewart (still only a Colonel) I tried to keep the oncoming Yeti at bay with my firearm.

I also ran with Jamie and the funny yet cowardly Evans as they were trapped in the dark by the oncoming web-like fungus that killed all in its path.

Instantly, *The Web of Fear* became my favourite book. It was more thrilling than *James and the Giant Peach*, better than those quaint and boring *Pudding Lane* books we were forced to read from time to time. I loved it so much. No other book had sucked me into its contents with such ease. I had given in and I was powerless to stop it from taking me over.

Maybe it was the influence of the Great Intelligence that seduced me! I just had to know what happened next. I couldn't put it down. Even after reading time was over, I wanted to stop my work that afternoon, sit under the shady tree in the playground and lose myself until the very last word had been read.

But, to guarantee that I completed it, I had to smuggle the book out of the class and back home.

Cunningly, looking from side-to-side, I slipped the book into my blue folder. My friend, Robin, spotted what I was doing but I knew he had my back. He was my most loyal friend and I knew that he wouldn't squeal. Later on, I would have an attack of conscience and put that brilliant novel back on the shelf. Time after time, over the next two years at that school, it was my go-to book. I read it and re-read it and memorised every word. I knew Anne Travers like she was family. I knew who the traitor was and was able to decipher Staff Sergeant Arnold's treachery before his motives were revealed to the rest of the characters.

I was so shocked that a book as brilliant as this was always there to be taken out, unwanted by my peers. What a treat they were missing out on. Eventually, I had taken the book out so often that it felt like the school was borrowing it from me.

You may be wondering why I admitted that I had taken that brilliant book out on 'extended loan.' Well, as I sit in my office writing this very book, nearly twenty years on, there it is, sitting proudly on my bookshelf, battered and torn more than ever but with some added text on its first page that was not there all those years ago.

The text consists of four words, just four words that make this old and tired book all that more special to me.

TO HAYDEN – TERRANCE DICKS.

It is to this day, and always will be, my favourite.

CHAPTER FIVE
THE FACT OF FICTION

Every *Doctor Who* fan experiences that horrific, stomach churning moment when they look upon a long list of episodes that no longer exist.

It is almost a rite of passage for some, the occasion when an individual can be converted from fan to super fan, consumed by the mystery as to why so many hours of the Doctor's adventures were junked, thrown away and chucked out, unwanted like yesterday's chip paper.

To this day, so many of us try to get our heads around the chaos that led to our favourite show being destroyed. To think that our beloved *Doctor Who* was seen as an unworthy commodity is sacrilege to us all. However, lest we forget, the BBC, indeed television itself, was still a new medium taking tentative steps in a golden age of creativity and producing entertainment for the now, not the future.

How were the archivists at BBC Enterprises supposed to know that, the second they started despooling the film that housed *Fury from the*

CHILD OUT OF TIME

Deep or *The Massacre*, they would be depriving future generations of the joy and wonder of something truly unique and special? To this little boy, it really came as a massive shock.

My first glimpse into the world of the missing episodes came when I visited a local newsagents on the high street. It was here where I blissfully flicked through the pages of *The Beano*, *The Simpsons Comic*, *The Dandy* and of course *Doctor Who Magazine* (*DWM*). More on that story, later.

As my parents were usually very kind and bought me a copy of each, which wasn't that expensive at the time but would probably cost you a lot more now, I knew I had to be on my best behaviour and receive my reward of a lovely new comic to indulge in whilst eating a fresh pack of Fizzy Jerkz and drinking Coke through a silly straw.

From time to time, I would venture into a cavern of books in the corner of the shop. I never found anything I liked. Books by Jane Austen, some buildings in a place called Rome and autobiographies from once famous personalities like Michael Barrymore abounded on the shelves.

But, on this occasion, I found something lying on top of the bargain bin that was right up my street.

It was called *The Doctor Who Yearbook* and had an unknown still of the TARDIS in what to me looked like a haunted wood, with tiny square boxes containing an image of each of the Doctors up until Sylvester McCoy.

Despite the optimism that I'd found yet another piece to fill the gaps in my *Doctor Who* jigsaw, I was apprehensive about what the pages held. The term 'yearbook' seemed to suggest that this would be nothing more than a calendar. I was wrong.

It was full of lists, so many captivating and intriguing lists. Each season was recorded in meticulous detail. I finally learned the name of the very first story, *100,000 BC*.

I always thought that the first story would be named something along the lines of 'The Birth of Doctor Who' or even as exciting as 'The Adventure Begins'.

Thank god I wasn't in at the tone meetings back then otherwise Sydney Newman and Verity Lambert would have had me sacked and banned from ever working for the BBC again!

Something like *100,000 BC* inspires curiosity, as did many other titles in those seasonal lists. Those that stuck out like shining beacons to me back then were coincidentally also the story names that I was unable to pronounce.

There was *Logo-police*, *Fronty-oze*, and *Castrovalva* (which promptly earned me a lunchtime detention for my first attempt at pronouncing it - thanks, Christopher H Bidmead). One of the greatest things about that yearbook was its record of dates on which certain episodes were recorded and broadcast. There was also a key allowing me to unearth the production code of *The Daemons*, see who'd written the story and pause to wonder whether its title was in fact a typo. And so, I studied. I made that book my bedtime reading for the next few nights, examining the pages whilst holding my bed covers up with my *Captain Scarlet* doll and using my Mickey Mouse torch to revise. If I'd worked as hard on my GCSE exams as I did with that book, I probably would have got all A's in my finals!

I burrowed myself into what was essentially a recorded history of days gone past and a TV show that no longer existed. It seemed so long since *The TV Movie* had aired, although it had probably been no more than 18 months but, at that age, that seemed like an eternity to me.

It was the discovery of the yearbook that started me off on that hobby of all Doctor Who fans. I started making lists. I used my school ruler to make dividers in my notebook and began cataloguing. I started with the name of the story, which season it was made in and who the companions were. I used a different colour for every Doctor so that I could tell that stories apart by each incarnation of my favourite Time Lord.

I no longer have the notepad, much to my regret, but I remember using red for William Hartnell, blue for Patrick Troughton, purple for

Tom Baker and then yellow for Peter Davison because it went with the colour of his hair. By the time I got to Sylvester McCoy's era, I'd run out of all other colours except silver, which seemed highly appropriate as he apparently had a story called *Silver Nemesis*.

For a child who delighted in disorganised chaos, this began an almost obsessive fascination with long lists for things that I loved. I wallowed in the knowledge I'd started to gain. Now I knew which story followed which and how many stories certain Doctors had done. I was even able to put a little check box in place so that I could put a tick next to a story I had seen.

At this point in my fandom, my viewed story count was a measly handful of oddities from the Second through to the Fifth Doctors. Certain stories seemed to gain a mythical air purely through their naming. But others were more explicit in revealing which monster the Doctor would be fighting. Titles like *Terror of the Autons*, *Revenge of the Cybermen* and *Revelation of the Daleks* more than gave the game away and ruined the mystery of who the big-bad might be. But others were more inscrutable. Titles like *The Ambassadors of Death*, *The Creature from the Pit* and *Ghost Light* really caught my eye.

Little details within the narrative text, which told the story of production and the goings-on behind the scenes and when the show was featured on another TV programme, such as *Blue Peter* or *Crackerjack*, were utterly fascinating.

However, my young mind was still easily confused by some of the words on the page. When the writer explained that the Daleks gave the new Second Doctor a 'baptism of fire' I thought that Patrick Troughton was literally surrounded by a flaming font! But I loved the inner sleeve pictures of the TARDIS set, and the discovery of one that looked like it was made from oak. I wondered which Doctor used that console room to travel around in time and space.

I was surprised to see just how few stories involved Colin Baker and Sylvester McCoy but I was already developing a bias against both the Sixth and Seventh Doctors purely on the calibre of their costumes. They just looked stupid to me back then. McCoy's looked okay, it was passable and I liked his umbrella. In fact, I wanted one with a question mark handle myself. But his jumper that resembled the outcome when knitwear gets splattered by a question mark gun was far too over the top. As for Baker's costume, it was like a rainbow had been violently sick on the poor man.

This bias meant that I decided to leave my search for their stories to the very last. There were so few clues to some stories but the pictures within the yearbook allowed me the chance to see what a Silurian looked like and who the Rani was. I thought her TARDIS was miles ahead of the

Doctor's on my personal spectrum of coolness and that Kate O'Mara's pose made her look very feline.

If this book wasn't heaven enough, there were also two comic book stories, *Star Beast II* and *Junkyard Demon II*. The former storyline saw the Doctor take on a white rabbit-like foe called The Meep in a cinema complex. As a villain, I thought that the Meep was fine in cartoon form but I hoped I wouldn't see him in the series.

As for *Junkyard Demon II*, I was perplexed as to why Lovejoy had popped up in Doctor Who. Again, the Fourth Doctor appeared and I thought that a shame. It would have been nice to see one of the others take on an Ian McShane impersonator and an army of Cybermen. I was also delighted to see that even in the years that it had been off the screen, *Doctor Who* was still active.

It was here that I discovered something called *The New Adventures*. I vaguely remembered seeing something similar on the shelves in that library in Haverhill, but they looked so different to the Doctor Who books I was reading, I thought that, if they were not Target books, they were not actually considered proper *Doctor Who*.

To my utter astonishment, the comprehensive text within this book alluded to a couple of Dalek movies that were produced in the 1960s and which featured neither William Hartnell nor Patrick Troughton!

CHILD OUT OF TIME

Just as I thought I was beginning to know the ins and outs of the show, yet another secret aspect to its long and rich life was revealed to me. I asked my parents to track the films down for me. As these were bonafide movies, I thought I would stand a better chance in finding them than I had in finding old stories.

Almost as surprising was the passage announcing that previously missing *Doctor Who* episodes were found after the BBC had initially mislaid them at one of their film storage facilities. Something called *The Ice Warriors*. I ran my fingers a couple of pages back and noticed that *The Faceless Ones* Episode 3 and *The Evil of the Daleks* Episode 2 had also been discovered. I didn't understand. Is this what Jon Pertwee meant by the Troughton years being 'cut back'?

Suddenly, to my horror, it dawned upon me. Doctor Who was not complete. Some of it was missing. Some of it, by the way in which this yearbook was worded, might never be found again.

I couldn't help but think just how unfair this news was. Now I had yet more questions circling my head like the Bohemian Rhapsody-style regeneration of the Second Doctor in *The War Games*. How much was missing? What stories were affected? I now knew that *The Abominable Snowmen* and *The Enemy of the World* were almost lost to the great junkyard in the sky, but what about the colour episodes? And, to my terror, what if one of the Doctor's regeneration stories was missing? I comforted myself by remembering that I'd seen all of the regenerations, meaning they must all survive.

Then I remembered Jon Pertwee's words and that the regeneration scene from Hartnell to Troughton was the only remaining material of that final episode of *The Tenth Planet*. Had great chunks of the Doctor's past really detached themselves like melting icebergs?

Soon after, my worst fears were realised. On a trip to Bury St Edmunds in Suffolk, we stopped off for a rummage through a bookshop on the High Street. There I encountered yet another Doctor Who reference bible, *The Television Companion*. It was an inexhaustible compendium of facts, quotes and reviews for every single story up until *The TV Movie*. I bought it with my pocket money and knew I was going to be well-informed after reading it cover to cover – especially as it was written by David J Howe and Stephen James Walker, who had written the Sixties, Seventies and Eighties books that by now I had either borrowed from the library or had at home thanks to some very generous presents from family members. How little they knew that they were fast becoming my enablers in this obsession with *Who*.

Then as I rummaged to the back of the book, I discovered a chapter entitled *Availability Checklist*. Whilst poring over every story title, my eyes darted to the right of the page where, to my relief, the word ALL adorned every story from the Pertwee era onwards. With a breath deeper than Loch Ness, I turned the page to check the Sixties output.

Thankfully, it looked like most of the First Doctor's run was safe and sound in the BBC Archives, all except something called *Marco Polo* and the curiously named *The Reign of Terror*. Then I discovered just how decimated Season Three had become. Just three stories now stood complete and brilliantly christened adventures such as *Galaxy 4*, *The Massacre of St Bartholomew's Eve* and *The Savages* were all gone and just two episodes of *The Daleks' Master Plan* had been saved from the edge of destruction. It was a shame to see the confirmation of missing episodes in that brilliant book, but then my heart sank even further.

Words failed me when I saw just how little of the Patrick Troughton years still existed. I was dismayed. His debut story *The Power of the Daleks* had been totally exterminated. Jamie's debut story *The Highlanders* had been sent to the gallows and was no more. Victoria's final story *Fury from the Deep* had been lost to the murky depths of time.

I couldn't quite believe what I was seeing. I would have sworn blind that the BBC would have saved the Daleks episodes and some of the more prominent monster adventures that made *Doctor Who* so special.

And then, I gulped hard and felt more disappointed than I had ever been about *Doctor Who*. There, in black and white were the words, *THE WEB OF FEAR* with a solitary '1' next to it. Only one episode existed. Just one. It was the first, which to me felt a little bit like a cruel joke.

Looking at the Yeti classic's fellow incumbents in Season Five, my crest fell even further. *The Abominable Snowmen* was also represented by just one instalment. *The Enemy of the World* (whoever he or she was) also had only one. *The Wheel in Space* (which to me sounded like a real B-Movie story, and I don't think I was far off there) was survived by just two. Thank god *The Tomb of the Cybermen* was complete. At least I had a chance of seeing that one someday.

When I took the book home, I knelt on the floor and drew up a list of missing episodes (by Doctor) and used my dad's calculator to tally up just how many were gone. For a kid who hated Maths and loathed doing his sums to the point he would want to throw a tantrum, I was very meticulous in my research.

Sitting back on my heels, I looked down at the figure on the digital screen of the calculator:

110 MISSING OUT OF 253.

CHILD OUT OF TIME

The realisation that my quest to watch every single *Doctor Who* story would never be fulfilled was crushing. I was appalled. How could the BBC do this to me? Why would they do this? What reason did the bigwigs at Television Centre have for destroying so much *Doctor Who*?

The thought that perhaps the show had been targeted because it had been cancelled and was now, in my mind, unpopular with the viewing public, made sense in my young head. I knew nothing about *Doctor Who* being one of many TV classics to have been purged due to lack of money, resources, space and, more importantly, foresight. I did think that maybe it had been picked on in this way because it was now off the air. But it had never crossed my mind that maybe these films were destroyed decades ago. That these black and white gems didn't even exist when I was born.

This news called for plausible ways of finding my way through those lost stories. Back then, I knew that my infrequent purchasing of *Doctor Who Magazine* (*DWM*) gave me a glimpse of something called 'telesnaps', visual windows into stories brilliantly captured by photographer John Cura. But I just thought that Cura had donated his pictures to the magazine in a loving gesture to show off his photography skills! I had no idea that these tiny snippets of off-air moments of certain episodes taken at the time of broadcast were the only visual representations of the lost stories that existed.

I certainly hadn't a clue that some fans had been diligent enough to record reel-to-reel audio recordings of every Sixties story.

So, for now, until I had read them all in Target book form, there was only one way to fill in the gaps left by those that I saw as mercenaries at the BBC. I had to fill in the blanks myself.

It was around this time that my love of *Doctor Who* had began to bleed into the stories that I was writing for my own amusement. Adventures that had frequently been had by Captain Kirk and Mr Spock, the Tracey Brothers or even Scrooge McDuck and bizarrely Oasis and the Spice Girls (the last might owe to the fact that I had a crush on Geri 'Ginger Spice' Halliwell at the time!) were now being had by the Doctor and his companions.

I distinctly remember scribbling away in my notebook on a holiday trip to a zoo in Bournemouth. Whilst everybody else was watching penguins jumping through hoops, I was sat alone on a mock-iceberg, scribbling away trying to imagine what might have happened during the last episode of *The Evil of the Daleks*.

Sad, I know, but the image of me sitting there in my little bubble of creativity was captured forever by a family member taking a picture of me, possibly at the precise moment I started blowing up Skaro in my head!

Another way of plugging the gaps was to act out scenarios with my sister and cousins. Clara was always Zoe, mainly because her bob haircut at the time resembled the one Wendy Padbury had in the late Sixties, and my younger cousin, Mike, was Jamie. He'd loved the few episodes that he'd seen.

Mike's exposure to *Doctor Who* was sparked by a 'boy's day out' trip to Peterborough where, in HMV, we found a row of *Doctor Who* videos. The ones that attracted both of us were the Cybermen covers.

I only had a certain amount of spending money and so faced a moral dilemma. Whether to buy *The Tomb of the Cybermen* or *Cybermen: The Early Years* I plumped for the latter because logic dictated that, as it had two episodes from two stories (in this case Episodes 2 and 4 of *The Moonbase* and Episodes 3 and 6 of *The Wheel in Space*), PLUS clips from *The Tomb of the Cybermen*, I would be getting more for my money.

Mike decided to get something totally unrelated to *Doctor Who* in the end but, when we retired to his house later that day, we watched in awe that first surviving episode of *The Moonbase*. It was atmospheric, dark, mysterious and very exciting. Jamie had been struck down with what we'd been told by the misinformed Colin Baker (the presenter of the tape) was a 'mystery illness'.

Ben and Polly were great companions to a more serious Second Doctor than I had seen before.

The suspicious and fearful crew of the Moonbase were also brilliant, with Hobson looking a little like my grandad. But, more than anything, the Cybermen were outstanding. Emotionless killers silently stalking proceedings.

Even if they were not on the screen, you could feel their presence throughout. Little wonder considering the climax to that part was the discovery that a Cybermen had been hiding in the sickbay all along.

What made *The Moonbase* even more thrilling for me was that it was the first time I had watched an episode having previously read it. Finally, I had something tangible to set alongside the prose. I noticed subtle changes between screen and book but nothing too substantial. And what's more, Mike loved it.

I don't know what it was that hooked him in. Was it the Doctor? The companions? The Cybermen themselves? All I knew was that finally, I had a playmate. Someone to share my obsession with. And in return, as we both shared a passion for football, I'd perhaps listen to him waxing lyrical about the wonders of Coventry City Football Club a little more. As long as he allowed me to justify my reasons as to why Tottenham Hotspur were the best club in the Premier League!

CHILD OUT OF TIME

So, it didn't take much to convince both Mike and Clara to become my trusted companions. I would usually pretend I was either Patrick Troughton, Tom Baker or Peter Davison's Doctors. Occasionally, my friend from school, Charlotte, would be roped in to play Polly (on account of her blonde hair). We would rush around the village and its picturesque fields and without fail our adventures would culminate with an attack of Daleks or Cybermen.

We would run for our lives back to the TARDIS (for practical reasons, I pretended that I'd fixed the chameleon circuit and it was presently manifested, to the minutest detail, as my bedroom) and then set the controls for more adventures until it was time to go home for tea.

But something was missing from my make believe wonderland - an eight-sided central console. But how could I replicate the one that I'd seen on the TV screen and occasionally in my dreams?

Firstly, I used the picture of the 1980s console on the front sleeve of the *Doctor Who* yearbook as a visual guide. Then, I started collecting bottle tops, pieces of cardboard that could bend and bits and pieces found in my Nan's kitchen. Straws, plastic cartons, you name it. From nothing but junk, I started constructing something pretty special.

Imagine what wonders I could have conjured had I been let loose in I. M Foreman's junkyard!

My arts and crafts teacher would have been proud. All these make-believe instruments were super glued onto an old box that bent in half to form an arch.

Try as I might, I didn't have the time or space for an eight-sided console, so two would have to do. It wasn't even a greyish cream colour like the one that the Doctor used but brown instead, but I didn't care.

To finish it off, I made a lever out of corrugated cardboard that flopped up and down to act as the door-opening mechanism. And in my head it all worked with the addition of some sound effects made by the person operating the console. Okay, so the central column didn't go up and down and was made out a long tube of toilet paper but it was structurally integral to the console!

Soon, many of my friends, including those who were not interested in the show, were clamouring to come around and play with my artwork. It was a great pivot for leverage to introduce more friends to *Doctor Who*.

Now my love for this long dead programme was alive and kicking. And in the back of my mind I was already becoming resigned to the fact that there was too much *Doctor Who* and not enough time or resources to watch it all. But it had given me yet another outlet. I was now playing *Doctor Who* with friends. And what's more, they were enjoying it!

At school, after a successful Show and Tell in which I did a ten minute skit on my now burgeoning collection of Target books and videos, their interest was palpable.

Afterwards, my class came up to the table and were thumbing through the books, picking up the videos and reading the blurb on the back. I genuinely couldn't believe it. Maybe my talking about *Doctor Who*, playing it and now the inclusion of the homemade console had done enough to convince them.

It was enough to prove that there was life in the old dog yet. *The TV Movie* may have been but a fleeting glimpse for the general public but it was the spark for me. And now, that spark had the potential to become a wildfire!

CHAPTER SIX
THE CELESTIAL TOYROOM

1999 was certainly the year that my boyish fandom for *Doctor Who* peaked. For just over 12 months, it felt like the show became the overwhelming factor in my young life. I was engulfed by a tidal wave of the fantastic worlds and adventures of the Doctor, sowing a love that I don't think has ever been matched.

Another prominent programme throughout my youth was *Blue Peter*. I'd watched it with my mother for years and my sister Clara and I would tune in every Monday, Wednesday and Friday to the world's longest running children's TV show. Every Christmas, the presenters would act out a pantomime and make an Advent Crown. My parents would snigger at their memories of this crude tinsel wrapped around four coat hangers going up in flames in previous years. I just remember feeling a warm glow when an army of schoolchildren roughly my age would burst through the big studio doors, singing *Hark the*

Herald Angels Sing until the obligatory final shot of the nativity scene finally filled the screen.

But that Christmas, the *Blue Peter* team of Stuart Miles, Katy Hill and Konnie Huq at this point had something special up their sleeves. And it wasn't a year's supply of sticky back plastic for every viewer.

The team were embarking on an adventure in space and time, taken through each other's Christmases of the past, present and future by an effervescent Mark Curry as some kind of weird Doctor-hybrid of a ginger Colin Baker married with the breathlessness of Peter Davison. This special was called *Back in Time for Christmas* and featured many former presenters in guest roles, including Peter Duncan as an all singing, all dancing Father Christmas. To be honest, I rather liked it but, looking back on it recently, I cringed so much at the cheesiness on display it took me two hours to prise my eyes open after assuring them that the horror was over.

However, I did allow myself a chuckle at a *Doctor Who* reference so blatant I'm surprised I didn't pick up on it back in the day. In one scene, Mark Curry's character goes off to rescue a teenage Konnie from a festive house party and leaves Stuart, resplendent as a Nativity shepherd, sitting on top of the time machine (well, I say time machine, it looked more like a fruit machine!)

Whilst Stuart awaits his friends, a policeman, played by John Leslie, stumbles upon the time machine on his beat and is startled when it dematerialises. In my mind I thought that this was a homage to Reg Cranfield's uncredited role as the Police Constable investigating the junkyard at the start of *An Unearthly Child*.

This wasn't to be the last nugget of *Doctor Who* imagery in *Blue Peter*. More was to come in the New Year.

In the build-up to the last year of the millennium, I'd received three items at Christmas that really surprised me. In the pile of presents, were three plastic action figures. To my excitement, they were *Doctor Who* action figures! Sadly, not one of the Doctor as I would have liked but small facsimiles of a painfully thin Cyberman, K-9 and a sinister-looking Davros more than made up for there being no Tom Baker toy.

I loved being able to express the *Doctor Who* of my imagination through play, something that I was still all too happy to do at the age of ten.

However, I was still having to use an amalgamation of action figures from other franchises. The band of make-believe heroes was made up of mostly *Thunderbirds*, *Captain Scarlet* and *Star Wars* figures and each was allotted the part of a character I'd seen or read about.

Princess Leia in her slave outfit was Leela, Captain Blue was the Fifth Doctor and a bearded Captain Black was employed to take up the role of the Anthony Ainley version of the Master. Jeff Tracey was occasionally called upon to stand in for William Hartnell whilst the male companion duties were shared between Luke Skywalker and Gordon Tracey as Jamie McCrimmon and Turlough respectively.

Certain baddies from extended multiverses also had a go at being villains from *Doctor Who*. I had an alien that I bought at a car boot sale that was orange and blobby and that became a Zygon (although I had yet to see their only television appearance) and Jabba the Hutt played a vastly overgrown version of Sil. But something was still missing from my growing carnival of monsters. A Dalek. Once again, the Doctor's greatest of enemies was proving to be an elusive entity. But all of that was to change soon after Christmas.

After a family shopping trip around Newmarket in Cambridgeshire, Clara and I found ourselves in a Toymaster's branch. And there, lying in the bargain bin was a Dalek. And not just any old Dalek. This one opened up and inside housed a play set, similar to the *Polly Pocket* ones my sister had, which included a tiny figure of the Fourth Doctor and what looked like Davros in a roll-on deodorant container. I was, of course, ecstatic and used some of my Christmas money to pay for it.

In the car on the way home, I remember tearing at the sharp plastic packaging and gnawing at it like a dog with a chew toy. My mother was concerned about me losing some of the parts in the dark, as the cold, wintery day had given way to the evening.

Of course, I wasn't going to lose any of the parts. I adored the play set. That little silvery Dalek sat proudly on my mantelpiece. For hours, I would crack it open like an Easter egg, play with the miniature Doctor and Dalek inside and always forget to close the TARDIS doors and lower the canon so, when I finished with it, the Dalek almost looked like a car with its hood up.

Now that my toy collection was beginning to expand, I started flicking through magazines and catalogues desperately looking for more. I dreamed of having a figure of every Doctor to play with and my favourite companions. I even started noticing more *Who* related toys in books I'd had for ages, such as the Eighties book by David J Howe, Mark Stammers and Stephen James Walker.

When I saw the image of a TARDIS play set, I pleaded with my parents to get it for me. But, sadly, they explained to me that it was made before I was born and that they had never seen it in the toy shops.

CHILD OUT OF TIME

Those three figures and the Dalek play set were to be the only *Doctor Who* toys I ever had as a child. But, boy, did I cherish them! The less I had meant the more I looked after them. I had lots of toys from my other favourite films and TV shows but the very fact that my *Doctor Who* toys and videos only made a modest pile made them that extra bit special. And 1999 wasn't only a golden year for toys. There was new *Doctor Who* on the television at last.

Firstly, as my schoolmates and I were preparing to run stalls at our local Comic Relief fundraiser that year, I was overjoyed to hear that a special *Doctor Who* episode was going to be shown during the telethon. And, what's more, Mr. Bean was going to play the Doctor!

I remember feeling a little bit sorry for Paul McGann as it seemed to me that he had been written out too soon. Of course, I wasn't aware that this was a spoof on my beloved show. I read about the build-up in that month's *DWM* and, although I merely skimmed through the main article and looked more at the pictures, I was totally flummoxed that there would be others playing the Doctor and couldn't wait to see how the story panned out on the night.

When the evening finally arrived, I sat and waited with bated breath for what I hoped was going to be a special and memorable moment in my *Doctor Who* fandom.

What I remember, however, was a broken down parody of how people remembered *Doctor Who*. Endless running down the same corridors, unexplained resolutions to complicated bits of science and the rivalry between the Doctor, played by the charming Rowan Atkinson, and the Master, played by Jonathan Price, or, as I knew him, the guy who was neither Anthony Ainley or Eric Roberts.

Another aspect I wasn't keen on was the love story between the Doctor and his companion, Emma, as played by Julia Sawalha who I recognised from Absolutely Fabulous. I disliked seeing the Doctor kissing a girl, especially as I perceived it as Mr Bean snogging Saffy. Also I'd never seen the Doctor as a romantic. Even with the Eighth Doctor locking lips with Grace in *The TV Movie*, I'd seen enough of the previous incarnations of my hero to understand that the Doctor was an asexual being, centuries-old and wise beyond the human conception of love.

And yet, despite this, I was willing to forgive the writer (some bloke called Steven Moffat, as I had discovered in *DWM*) because he gave me Daleks. Lots of Daleks!

The moment that the Doctor and Emma ran into a room full of CGI imaginings of the Time Lord's greatest foes and that screech pierced the living room, I discovered a feeling that the show had never given me before. It was a feeling shared by my classmates as, when I went to school the next day, the sight of Daleks all shouting, 'EXTERMINATE!' was the talk of the playground. Oh, how the parents who had grown up in the Sixties and Seventies must have smiled hearing so many children impersonating Skaro's finest.

'Oh, my god! What's going to happen next!' I cried. For the first time, I didn't know where the plot was going to take me next. No idea of how the Doctor and his friend were going to get out of it. I hugged my knees to my chest as I awaited the fourth and final part of this oddly engaging story. And then...

'Right, bed time!'

I turned around in astonishment. Surely my parents were not going to send me off to bed at such a crucial stage of the story. I looked up at the clock on the mantelpiece. It had gone well past 9pm and my curfew had fallen.

As I trudged off to bed with the assurance that my parents would tape the final part, I was fuming. It was a Friday and there was no school the next day so why on Earth did I have to turn in now? Every time I got close to indulging in my favourite show, it felt like it was being taken away from me.

Resentfully, I slipped between my bed covers, closed my eyes and crossed my fingers that the VHS recorder didn't go belly up.

The next morning, the first thing I did was to jump downstairs and ask to watch the concluding chapter. After brushing my teeth and getting some breakfast, I wound the tape back to the correct spot, remaining hopeful that the Doctor would triumph over the Daleks and sort the Master out once and for all. What I got instead was bafflement beyond belief.

Why did the Master now have breasts? Why was the Doctor farting to warn his arch nemesis of "certain doop" (the line used by the Master in the special)? Why did he keep regenerating? And why was he now a woman? And why oh why was the fact that the sonic screwdriver had three settings anything to shout about? Sadly, I pressed stop on the remote and let my sister watch her early morning cartoons instead. What had started off as a wave of excitement had now crashed onto a shore of confusion. I had hated what I had seen. Especially the final shot of the new female Doctor (played by an actress I only knew as Patsy) and the Master walking off arm in arm. It might sound a little strong to say that I was disgusted but I think I was more disappointed than anything else.

I needn't have worried about finding my next *Doctor Who* fix, however, because it felt like the Doctor was always around now. I had more Target books and more videos than I could ever have dreamed. Recently, more titles had been added to my growing collection. I'd picked up

CHILD OUT OF TIME

The War Machines, *Planet of Fire* and *Revenge of the Cybermen* from video shops in the area, all of which I had grown to adore. I'd even started a revolutionary way of keeping old *Doctor Who* stories that I didn't own.

On a family trip to Dorset, I'd used another new Christmas gift, the *Talkboy*, to tape a few episodes of *The Simpson*s onto audio cassette. My methods were crude yet effective. Basically I just held the recorder up to the speaker grille on our rather modern 32" television and prayed that my family were quiet or my arm didn't get too tired.

Sometimes I would prop the mechanism up on a pile of books. My standard procedure would be to grab several of the newest *Blue Peter* annuals and use them. I never resorted to enlisting the first ten books as a plinth as they were far too old and I didn't want to damage them.

It occurred to me that, as my recent invention of taping audio off the TV had proved successful, I could try to convert my videos into cassettes.

My parents would occasionally do the same thing with Disney videos. With their fingers hovering over the pause and record button, they would try to isolate the music tracks from movies such as The Lion King and Pocahontas for my sister to listen to on long trips in the car.

As I was still very young and didn't know how to operate the tape recorder, I used my tried and tested method of the *Talkboy* standing on a pile of

Blue Peter annuals as close to the speakers as possible for the desired effect.

The first time I did this with a *Doctor Who* video was round at my friend, Charlotte's, house. She is one of my oldest and most loyal friends so naturally I had attempted to brainwash her with my love for the show. And, to some degree, my enthusiasm had rubbed off on her. Indeed, she was the first person to come over and play with my homemade TARDIS console!

With Charlotte's help, I managed to record the first two episodes of *Planet of Fire*. Although I would watch the episodes whenever I could (well, whenever I was allowed to), I couldn't wait to go to bed that night and listen back to the recording.

As darkness descended and my eyes became heavy, I lay back in my bed and popped my headphones on. I can still hear the hum of the static from the recording now. I yelped as the BBC ident shattered the silence and then relaxed again as the tape once again faded into nothingness. I then yelped even higher just moments later as the theme tune screeched in.

I'd been careful to include a particular advertisement for *Doctor Who* on the tape because I loved the look of it. If you owned a copy of the *Planet of Fire* video, dear reader, then you'll know which advert I'm talking about. It featured clips of all of the Doctors starting with William Hartnell and finishing with Sylvester McCoy and it also (and most vitally) included a short scene of every regeneration. I marvelled at it. Even in audio form, hissing through the crackly sound coming from my Toshiba headphones, it gave me goose bumps.

After the reassuring sound of the TARDIS materialising, I was alone again in the darkness. Then the third yelp was the loudest as the Peter Davison titles crashed into my ears. I quickly pressed pause as I could hear my Dad running up the stairs. He burst into my room, startled and wanting to see if I was okay. I assured him that I was just making noises because I was having a weird dream. After all, it must have been 11 o'clock at this point so, if he caught me listening to my Walkman, then I was for the high jump! My mum also hated me listening to it before I went to sleep due to the slight chance that I might garotte myself with the headphone cord in my sleep. And she may have had a point given the number of times I've woken up with the cord threatening to throttle me.

I knew that this secret listening malarkey was risky business, so I took two precautions. One, I turned the volume down and two, I placed my head between my two pillows to muffle any sound escaping.

Eventually, I snuggled down to two episodes of squabbling, accusations of Logar being a myth, Kamelion seemingly sabotaging the TARDIS and Turlough being secretive. Alas,

With with this being on audio, I had to settle for only imagining Peri in her bikini.

However, the audio quality left a lot to be desired. I could make out the action, that was fine, but the persistent rustling and audible chatter in the background from Charlotte's mum on the phone was more than a little annoying.

Soon after, I plucked up the courage to ask my parents if I could use their technique of recording the sound direct from the VCR. Happily, they showed me how they did it.

I discovered that a cable from the Hi-Fi system led all the way down into the back of the TV and video recorder, meaning all I had to do was press record on the cassette player inside the Hi-Fi and then everyone could make as much noise as they wanted and it wouldn't affect my recording.

Around this time, I was again raiding Haverhill Library as another tranche of *Doctor Who* videos had arrived. I rented out *The Hartnell Years*, *The Dalek Invasion of Earth* (Episodes 4-6) and *The TV Movie*, which I hadn't seen since its original transmission. I had found it profoundly random that one tape included just one half of a story, but it looked really old so I just assumed that the VHS runtime couldn't meet the demands of a six-part story.

Gleefully, I watched all three. I loved *The Hartnell Years* tape because, much like its *Troughton Years* counterpart, it was a trip into new and mysterious waters for me. I loved the pilot, how spooky and mysterious it was and immediately added that and the only surviving episode of *The Crusade* (not for long!) to my audio library for safe keeping.

The Dalek Invasion of Earth, however, was disappointing. I didn't have a clue what was going on, and the Doctor, barring a sudden fall at the start of *The End of Tomorrow*, wasn't as prominent as I wanted him to be. I watched the remaining two parts but it was a very sunny day and my mind was elsewhere. It's surprising when I look back now but the Daleks hadn't truly captured my imagination as much as the Cybermen had a year previously.

Despite this underwhelming feeling, I recorded them all as I watched them, carefully flipping the cassette when it reached the 45 minute mark after two episodes. As these were C-90 cassettes that the family owned, I had the pleasure of putting a whole four-part story on one tape. Longer stories that I owned such as *The Green Death* had to be put to one side and, sadly, were never recorded. Quite how that pilot episode of *An Unearthly Child* ended up on a tape that also included all of the music from the Disney film, *Hercules*, remains a mystery to this day.

Now that I had yet another medium to store my borrowed tapes on, the *Doctor Who* library in my bedroom now outstripped my pile of *Simpsons* and *Beano* comics. It was fair to say that *Doctor*

Who was the most important show in my life.

Despite the genius of the show not affecting my friends as deeply, we were all about to get another treat as, one day (I forget if it was a Monday, Wednesday or Friday), just after teatime, my sister and I dived for the sofa for the latest installment of *Blue Peter*. As the trademark ship swang into view, my hair stood on end as the all-too-familiar screech of a *Doctor Who* cliffhanger filled the living room like audible gold. The next thing I knew, the time tunnel and the TARDIS from Tom Baker's era zoomed towards us accompanied by the theme music that usually accompanied William Hartnell's title sequence. Yes, even at that tender age, *Doctor Who* fandom was turning me into a pedant.

Then, one by one, a gallery of the Doctor's greatest villains was paraded before us. Some in colour, some in black and white, but each one unique and special. I thought the Drashigs looked amazing even though I had no idea who or what they were yet and cheered as my favourite monsters, the Cybermen, clomped their way into proceedings.

Before I had the chance to yelp the words 'MUM! *DOCTOR WHO* IS ON BLUE PETER!' the TARDIS materialised and, as it stood there fully formed, I wondered which Doctor was going to emerge from those doors that just begged to be pulled to open. Would it be the great man, Tom

Baker himself? Peter Davison? Colin Baker? Sadly, it was only Katy Hill, dressed as the Fourth Doctor, Stuart Miles, looking very dapper in the Fifth Doctor's cricket whites, and Konnie Huq, in what looked like the Eighth Doctor's garb but I couldn't be sure.

Agonizingly, the presenters moved on to another subject altogether in which I had no interest. But, within minutes, they were back, flanked by some monsters which I'd never seen before. My description of these alien rogues sounds now as surreal as they looked way back in 1999. There was a disgusting looking thing with a hood sitting by a computer, a grey figure that resembled a zombie and what looked like a potato wrapped in foil also sitting by another computer. Maybe they were browsing Encarta, I thought, for weaknesses of the human race in a bid to take over the planet from a children's television programme. Then the trio took us down Memory Lane and explained the whole concept of the show within the space of a couple of minutes.

They described who the Doctor was, where he came from, how old he was and how long his adventures were broadcast on television. I was loving every second if it. I couldn't stop grinning when some of the monsters were paraded down a catwalk in what to me resembled a galactic fashion show. But all the interplanetary monstrosities were blown away as soon as the

Daleks homed into view. What was it that was so special about these creatures? There they were looking as splendid as ever, threatening to exterminate Stuart Miles, much to the hilarity of my sister and me.

Despite my trouble trying to persuade my friends to give in to the *Doctor Who* bug, I was surprised to see that the computers that had once been occupied by baddies were now being used by children. They were using something called 'the internet' to browse for information on *Doctor Who*. I had heard of the internet. We had an Information Technology Centre in a room at my school but only one computer was connected to something called the World Wide Web and that's what these children were using. To look up *Doctor Who*! I sat in astonishment as one of the children said that his favourite Doctor was Patrick Troughton. 'Mine too!' I exclaimed.

Then Konnie Huq introduced a new face from inside the TARDIS. It was Rosetta from Eastenders. I had no idea that she'd also been in Doctor Who!

'Of course! It's Leela!'

I searched my memory for the actress's name before Konnie blew the answer and introduced Louise Jameson and a clip from one of her stories. 'I like her. I think from now on I need to look out for more of her videos!'

The enduring thought from this wonderful *Blue Peter* special was 'why aren't there any children like that at my school?' Why wasn't there anyone I could sit with who knew what a Zygon was? I had a couple of pals who indulged in my obsession but, occasionally, I thought it was more out of boredom and pity than acute fascination. Hopefully, there would be more fans after this than before and I would have someone to argue with about who were better, the Daleks or the Cybermen.

The icing on the cake for me was the moment when Stuart announced a competition for *Doctor Who* fans aged 15 or under. It was the chance to win lots of videos, many of which I didn't have. I scrambled for a pen and paper as I didn't want to go through the rigmarole of searching for the question again on *Blue Peter*'s ceefax page (page 555, if memory serves - how on Earth do I remember that little detail?).

The question itself, however, like the videos that once adorned my shelves, is now lost in the mists of time. After asking my parents politely if I could enter the competition and use the telephone to submit my answer, I had a phone call from my cousin, Michael. He told me that he'd entered the competition too. I was slightly miffed by this. What if he won it and I didn't? Wasn't I a bigger fan? In the end, we struck a bargain in which we would alternate weekend ownership of the tapes if one of us was lucky enough to win.

I was left exhilarated by the show and, what's more, the following Monday, more of my classmates were keen to question me on *Doctor Who*. By now it was common knowledge that I was a huge fan and, for another fleeting moment of schoolground popularity, *Doctor Who* was (just like yo-yos and Pokémon cards) in vogue again. However, it wasn't long before interest dwindled again. Just like after the broadcast of *The Curse of Fatal Death*, the short term memories of my classmates were soon occupied by something else that was less invigorating than the good Doctor.

A few months passed which seemed an eternity before an intriguing advert followed another glorious edition of *The Simpsons* on BBC2. Something was coming that was to round off 1999 with a bang. I was puzzled to see a girl on a sofa happily eating spaghetti hoops as an army of Daleks screamed off camera. Even stranger was the image of a lime jelly taking off like a rocket before the face of a balding, petrified man peeked over the back of the sofa. I knew what this was all about now.

To my delight, the best theme tune in the world heralded something special, and the announcer chillingly proclaimed, 'Behind the sofa…no-one can hear you scream…'

CHAPTER SEVEN
DOCTOR WHO NIGHT

Saturday. November 13th 1999

With the dawn of a new millennium breathing down our necks, my ten-year-old self was having the time of his life. My little world felt safe and wholesome. I had my family (with another on the way) my friends, my comics, my toys and my *Doctor Who* collection to keep me occupied as the threat of a 'Millennium Bug' loomed like a formless, shapeless being with a mind of its own. Of course, that description was lifted from the delightful pages of *Doctor Who and the Web of Fear* which continued to accompany me on trips to see family and, more importantly, to school in that battered folder in splendid TARDIS blue.

It had been over three years since I'd welcomed *Doctor Who* into my life and now the culmination of just over a third of my lifetime awaited me in the form of a celebratory night of programmes on BBC2. I'd been waiting for what seemed like an eternity for this night to arrive and now here it was. I was about to see a special night of all things Time Lord.

In the days building up to the telethon, I'd managed to coerce money from Mum and Dad to buy the latest *Doctor Who Magazine*. I hadn't always been able to afford what seemed to be the only outlet for news and features of a show that had been pretty much dead for more than a decade on television and eagerly peeled through the pages to see if there was any news of a brand spanking new series being put into production or if any long-lost episodes had been found but, sadly, 99.9% of the time, both seemed to be nothing but fierce dreams in my mind.

My first issue of *DWM* was purchased not long after the original transmission of *The TV Movie*. The cover photograph depicted Paul McGann as the Eighth Doctor and Daphne Ashbrook as Dr Grace Holloway, lurching over that brilliantly Victorian TARDIS console. Inside were two important articles that would go on to influence certain aspects of my growing fandom.

The first was a countdown list entitled *20 Moments When You Know You Are Watching the Greatest Television Show Ever Made*. These were 20 moments of mesmeric, influential and ultimately memorable scenes that, in *DWM*'s opinion, captured the very essence of what made *Doctor Who* great.

CHILD OUT OF TIME

I read about the time that the Seventh Doctor went toe-to-toe with a gunman and managed to overcome his assailant with the power of words, which suggested to me that reason and willpower can triumph over physical might and intimidation.

At the age of seven, you need to be told something like that as a way of reassurance that people who threaten you are really just scared themselves and hiding behind their threats. And since Sylvester McCoy looked small as the soldier rose above him, machine gun in his arms ready to pull the trigger, it taught me that the smallest man could also be the most powerful in the room.

I peered at the little panels that held screen captures of these iconic moments in the show's history and read about how Tom Baker's last words in the show were the bittersweet, 'It's the end...but the moment has been prepared for.' I saw the moment that two schoolteachers called Ian Chesterton and Barbara Wright burst through the doors of an old police box standing in a junkyard and learned from a strange old man and his unearthly granddaughter that it could move anywhere in time and space. I remember putting the magazine down after reading the whole article (which took some effort for a seven-year-old with the attention span of a disobedient Sontaran). 'I've got to watch more of this,' I phew-ed to myself as I leaned back against my bedroom radiator.

The second article that grabbed my imagination was a telesnap recounting of the sixth instalment of *The Evil of the Daleks*, their last adventure of the 1960s at the end of Patrick Troughton's first season as the Doctor.

It was the last three panels that excited me the most. The first showed the TARDIS being revealed to a captured Doctor, Jamie and Waterfield as they stood in front of the Emperor Dalek, whose imposing, frightening aura bled through the black and white image and into my consciousness. The second showed the Doctor's face, mouth open in shock, helpless as the Emperor orders him to deliver something called 'the Dalek Factor' throughout the history of Earth. And then, the last image was simply of the title card and it read, 'DIRECTOR – DEREK MARTINUS'. I marvelled at the absurdity of it all and couldn't wait for the next issue to discover the resolution to this intriguing cliff-hanger.

Despite the lack of the news, what I really wanted, of course, was brand new *Doctor Who* on the TV. *DWM* was my infrequent treat opening up the current goings on in the Whoniverse. The reason that my purchases were so sporadic was entirely down to scheduling. If *The Beano* or *The Simpsons Comic* came out in the same week, then my parents would be strict on their budget and limit my literary intake to just one a week. And because the one local newsagent which supplied it kept so few copies, I'd sometimes race to the shelf to find an empty space where the *DWM*s once sat.

So it goes without saying that, when a copy was in the shop and I was allowed to have it, I snatched it up like Stotz with a supply of spectrox. I adored the comic strip which continued the adventures of the Eighth Doctor and a companion I'd never met before called Izzy. Although the illustrations were in black and white (which I thought was wrong as this was now the 1990s and nothing was in black and white anymore) and the Doctor had regenerated into some bald stranger at the end of my very first comic strip, I was in my element. Especially when a friendly Cyberman, who went by the name of Kroton, briefly joined the TARDIS crew.

Whilst I had struggled to engage with the Doctor's eighth manifestation in novel form, I had no problems following his adventures in *DWM* as here he and his friends (and enemies) allowed me a visual representation of their world. I used to bastardise the comics from each issue and separate every single page into a ring binder with a see through wallet so I could collect an anthology and read the adventures as complete stories. Sometimes there would be a hole in the collection when I'd been forced to skip an issue, making that instalment instantly a missing episode. It's a shame really. Ten years on, I could have just bought the omnibus volumes that were reprinted by the good people at Panini Comics and kept my *DWM* issues intact.

In an age before the internet had infiltrated every home in the world like some weird form of creature intent on enslaving the human race through the miracle of broadband (ooh, that would make a good Doctor Who story – oh, Steven Moffat has already done that), *DWM* was my only window into what was going on.

It was there that I learned of the recovery of *The Lion* (the first part of the William Hartnell adventure, *The Crusade*) and moaned ungratefully that a Patrick Troughton episode hadn't been discovered instead.

Within one issue, I also read that Peter Davison, Colin Baker and Sylvester McCoy had recorded a new story for the show called *The Sands of Time* but my smile soon disappeared when I saw that it was only going to be on audio, produced by some company called Big Finish. But that won't work, I thought. Doctor Who should be on the telly, not on CD!

'It won't catch on,' I groaned, starting a record for predicting the future which remains rubbish.

In the particular issue of *DWM* that coincided with Doctor Who Night, I read on the *Gallifrey Guardian* news page that a new series of repeats was about to start on BBC2. I nearly wet myself in excitement! Finally, I was going to see these classic gems, starting with Jon Pertwee's debut,

CHILD OUT OF TIME

Spearhead from Space. I had never seen *Spearhead* before, despite my cousin Michael owning the video tape after purchasing it on a family trip to the BBC Experience at Broadcasting House, and I ringed the transmission date in the magazine as a reminder, although it was highly unlikely that I was going to forget it was on. BBC2 on weeknights was sacred for so many brilliant TV shows. And now *Doctor Who* was going to join them. Fantastic!

I read ahead to some spoilers for that Saturday night and learnt that Tom Baker had recorded some special scenes as the Doctor to introduce the programmes. What a treat to see the great Fourth Doctor in brand new material. There were going to be documentaries about the show and its monsters, some sketches from two blokes I'd never heard of called Mark Gatiss and David Walliams and a repeat of *The TV Movie*.

I was pleasantly surprised to read that a classic episode was also going to be shown. According to *GG*, the BBC had the option of broadcasting an episode from *The Daleks* (another one I hadn't seen) and the one that excited me the most, the only surviving instalment of *The Web of Fear*! I crossed my fingers and peered to see which one it was in that week's edition of the *Radio Times*, which excitingly carried a fantastic picture of a black Dalek surrounded by dry ice, taken by the photographer Lord Snowdon, and the ominous text, which read: 'Look WHO's back on Saturday night.'

The excitement was becoming all too much. Throughout that Saturday, the coming evening filled my every thought. Looking back now, it's clear to me that this was no longer just a hobby or interest in one of the greatest shows ever made. It was a full-blown addiction. Although my bedroom wall was dressed with all kinds of visual clues to my interests, there wasn't much in the way of *Doctor Who* posters as, back then I could never find any on sale. But the shelves were bulging with all kinds of merchandise from the show and there were always well-worn copies of *DWM* strewn across the carpet like lily pads on a lake of blue polyester.

The show wouldn't be starting until 9pm. So, what to do with my time before then? Sensibly, I decided to be as active as I could and played football down at my local park with some school chums. I remember thinking how canny this activity would prove to be. You see, my parents were both worried that, as I had a special dispensation to stay up longer than I ever had done previously, I would be tired and cranky the next day and that this would have a detrimental effect on my (and their) weekend. But as I wore myself out during the day BEFORE *Doctor Who Night*, I knew that I was going to crash and sleep well during the afternoon. And do you know what? My tactic worked!

CHILD OUT OF TIME

After my mid-afternoon snooze, I decided to do a little light reading (viz *The Robots of Death* novelisation from front-to-back) and then have another quick sleep after tea time and check that afternoon's football scores. My father then asked me if I'd like to accompany him to the supermarket to purchase some nibbles for the night. Fantastic! I got to stay up past my bedtime, eat crisps AND watch *Doctor Who*! What more do you want as a fan of ten?

After a jaunt to the local Sainsburys, and under strict instructions not to help myself to the various treats, I retreated upstairs to my room and donned my burgundy dressing gown and slippers in what soon became a ritual dress code whenever I watched *Doctor Who*. As my dressing gown was the same colour as the coat that Tom Baker wore in Season 18, I used to pull the belt out of the loops and wrap it around my neck in pale imitation of the great Fourth Doctor. It took about a year to grow out of that poor excuse of a cosplay.

So, resplendent in my do-it-yourself Fourth Doctor-style garb, I plonked myself firmly on the sofa for what promised to be a night of nostalgia and discovery. I sat there, flanked either side by my parents and waited, my patience stretched to breaking point. It all started with a Dalek in the shape of the BBC2 logo, which drew a chuckle from my dad. Then the night kicked-off with a brilliant monologue from Mr Baker in which he reminisced about meeting Cleopatra and what a woman she was and Helen of Troy ('she was a woman, too!')

The thing that struck me most was how much the now older actor looked like his predecessor, Jon Pertwee. The bouffant shock of white hair gave him more than a passing resemblance to the man he'd replaced in the TARDIS. However, although the winds of time had ravaged him, there was no doubt that this was the man that played a version of the Doctor that, at that age, I had taken into my heart.

What came next was a teaser of what the night was offering. There was a documentary called *An Adventure in Space and Time*, which was accompanied by a clip of the Fourth Doctor getting throttled by a piece of slimy plastic. Then there was something called *Carnival of Monsters* which I was looking forward to the most as it was a comprehensive look at the villains that had helped make the show one of the most imaginative and frightening on television. Then there was what looked like the comedy sketches I'd read about in the *Radio Times* followed by an announcement that the final episode of the very first Dalek adventure was to follow.

I confess that I was a little miffed at this. I'd pinned all my hopes on seeing the only surviving episode of *The Web of Fear*, a story which had gripped me and soon become my favourite from the power of its prose version alone. At this point,

I uncrossed my fingers and slouched. Oh well, I thought, at least the rest of it will be worth it.

It's hard for a hyperactive ten-year-old to be gripped by a documentary, something which is removed from the land of fiction and presented very much in the realm of fact. But, because this was a special *Doctor Who* edition I was watching, I made a bit of a game of it. The special was chock-a-block with clips and excerpts I'd never seen before and I dredged up all the *Doctor Who* knowledge from my memory, trying to match characters to names and stories to titles.

'Ooh, Davison. Cybermen. Adric. That must have been *Earthshock*. Man, that looks cool. And look, it's Patrick Troughton, Zoe and a guy who isn't Jamie but then again he is. That one's from *The Mind Robber*.'

My parents must have looked to one another and shook their heads in agreement. 'How is this kid ever going to get married?' True, it's only recently that anyone has been able to compete with my passion for a fifty-year old show but, at the age of ten, girls were far from my mind. Well, until a clip of Peri came up on screen, that is!

Although it wasn't as memorable as I'd hoped, there were several lines that will stay with me forever. There was Tom Baker's admission that he had the remarkable ability to make a grandmother's bosom tingle whenever they saw him. Peter Davison remarked that he thought that the superior visual effects of *Star Wars* contributed to Doctor Who's decline. There was Sylvester McCoy telling the viewer that he felt more suited to and capable in the role than ever before in his ten minute appearance in *The TV Movie*. More than anything else, I remember the voice of a rather dour costume designer declaring that the show had had its day as the technology was now so advanced that there was no way that a ropey, cheap-looking science fiction programme like *Who* would ever make its way onto our television screens again. I was rather miffed by that.

Here I was, a member of a missing generation, the first and only ever to have seen brand new *Doctor Who* in a serialised, continuous format and here was some old stiff telling me it would never come back. Who did he think he was? I bet he's kicking himself now!

I must admit that the sketches from Mark Gatiss and David Walliams went over my head at the time. I didn't have the know-how to grasp the hilarious irony of *The Web of Caves*. I just thought that, whichever alien foe Walliams was portraying (I thought it might be a Drahvin as he looked like he was wearing a skirt), it wasn't a very dangerous one. In fact, it was really rather annoying.

My highlight of the evening's entertainment was unequivocally the *Carnival of Monsters* retrospective. For what seemed like an hour, I marvelled at in-depth analysis of a whole host of enemies. Daleks, Cybermen, Voc Robots, Morbius, Sontarans - they were all here in all their villainous glory. I was rather shocked at how violent Morbius seemed to be, strangling the Doctor half to death with his crab-like claw. I also had no option but to gloss over the fact that the clip featuring Toberman killing a Cyberman in *The Tomb of the Cybermen* included what looked like a tissue box with shaving foam oozing from it as, deep down, I had to acknowledge that it looked fairly crap!

However, out of all of the monsters I wanted to see, the Autons looked the coolest. Their blank, expressionless faces, their guns concealed in their dead plastic hands, exploding out of shop windows and gunning down innocent civilians out early to do their shopping sent chills shivering all through my body. The only other monster I was as inquisitive about was the Sea Devils. To me, they were nothing short of menacing as they broke through the seabed and took on the British Navy with their guns that looked like CDs and spat fire as they attacked with deadly precision. I had to seek out their adventures and watch them as soon as possible!

Sadly, my enjoyment was ruined by my parents' insistence that it was time to go to bed. Now remember, in the build-up to *Doctor Who Night*, I'd consumed copious amounts of sweets, played football and enjoyed a well prepared nap.

So, by this point I wasn't feeling at all tired. Yet, just as the short film, *How To Build a TARDIS* started, I was toddling off to my bedroom, making sure that every stomp up the stairs was heard loud and clear by my mother and father as yet again their curfew had ruined my chance to indulge in more *Who* after dark. I remember thanking my stars that we lived in an age where home video recording was prevalent; otherwise I'd have missed that ancient episode of *The Daleks*.

I was more wide awake than I ever had been at 11 o' clock at night. So, as I heard Mum and Dad retire for the evening, I reached into my blankets, clutched my Walkman and listened to the first two episodes of *Death to the Daleks*. Suffice to say, I was soon sound asleep!

The next day, I settled down to watch that ancient and forever episode and found myself enraptured by this version of the Doctor yet still a bit cautious. I found Hartnell's features when shackled to the Dalek wall somewhat disconcerting. I was used to the Doctor being in control. The fact that he was even willing to bargain with the mutated monsters did little to convince me that this version of my hero was anything more than powerless in the face of adversity. If anything, the real hero of the piece was Ian Chesterton. As I grew up, I realised that this was intention all along, to have both Ian and Barbara be our real guides in the story. They were our eyes and ears in a black and white world and our windows into the adventure.

For the most part, I found this Dalek episode slightly confusing as I hadn't seen the rest of the adventure (even if the voice of the book from *The Hitchhikers Guide to the Galaxy* was on hand to fill in the blanks). But what really won me over with Hartnell's interpretation of the Doctor was his monologue at the very end of the story. When the camera focuses in on the Doctor after he speaks to Dyoni and Alydon about the future of the Thals on Skaro, he muses about the search for the truth of life.

'My journey is out there, in the stars. And yours is here.' I marvelled at the superb dialogue and the delightful way in which Hartnell delivered it. It spoke deeply to me about the future and the way in which everyone lives their lives in a different way. And, from that moment on, the First Doctor was okay in my book.

After that little taster of the first Dalek adventure, in which I'd describe my reaction to the Daleks themselves as tepid as I was still convinced that the Cybermen would always be better (thanks for blowing that one out of the sky, *Doomsday*), there was yet another skit in which David Walliams met Mark Gatiss in a sci-fi filled bedroom to introduce him to a new 'friend'.

The 'friend' in question, was a bound, gagged and startled-looking Peter Davison. Out of all of the comedy sketches performed that night, this was the one that made me laugh the most. I much preferred it to the two previous helpings as it actually starred a real Doctor and Davison's expressive, helpless mannerisms as he listened to the insane, fanatical conversation between his captors was fantastic. Plus, it helped to have a Doctor included that I liked and knew well.

Then, all of a sudden, the tape cut out. There was nothing else left on the recording. I was confused by this as I was sure that *The TV Movie* was to follow. I even looked back through the *Radio Times* to check. Unfortunately, Dad had picked up on my ambivalence towards Paul McGann's only on-screen adventure and decided that I wasn't that keen on it. Also, it wasn't practical to put a 90 minute show on top of a two hour theme night on a Maxell 180 minute tape. So, *The TV Movie* was not recorded. Some fans would call this a blessing but, as a completionist, I would have preferred to have it rather than not.

I wondered whether any of my school friends has seen the glut of programmes on BBC 2 that Saturday night. But, just in-case they hadn't, I decided that *Doctor Who* would be my topic of choice in Show and Tell that coming week. I really wanted to take in all of my videos and magazines but my parents thought that it might be better if I took only the video sleeves, a couple of *DWM* issues and my favourite books, and then only if I promised that I wouldn't lose them or give any of them out to my friends.

During my talk, in which I was aided by my friend, Robin, who stood there like an auctioneer showing off my *Doctor Who* goodies as I described what they were, the class was spellbound. Indeed afterwards, almost all of my classmates got up and started thumbing through my merchandise and asking to borrow bits and pieces. Eventually, I gave in and I lent my *Planet of Fire* VHS (the only one I'd smuggled out in its full physical form) to a boy in my year. My mum would have been furious but I did just get away with it.

So, once again, the curiosity of my peers meant that *Doctor Who* was still of interest amongst the youth of the day. It might not have been as popular as *The Simpsons*, *Buffy* or *Robot Wars* to them, but it was there, waiting in a less dormant state than before. But little did I know that my interest had reached its summit.

As retrospective nostalgia nights go, *Doctor Who Night* was a fantastic example of just how good this old show was and could be again. But now that I look back at it, although the whole evening's entertainment had filled that weekend like an impossible girl scattered through a time stream, it was as good as it could get for this member of the lost generation of fans. If anything, it was the crest of a wave that had built and built over the years between that first broadcast of *The TV Movie* and that weekend in late 1999. But as 2000 dawned, my life was about to change forever and that wave was about to crash, almost never to resurface again.

CHILD OUT OF TIME

CHAPTER EIGHT
THERE'S NO POINT IN BEING GROWN UP IF YOU CAN'T BE CHILDISH SOMETIMES

Before the magic of Doctor Who started to slip through my fingertips, I was to experience several more encounters with the worlds of my favourite Gallifreyan that would live long in my memory.

The final Christmas of the 20th century saw a Gribble family trip to the bright, wondrous lights of London. Back then, a trip to the big city, especially at the best time of the year for a child, always seemed like a big festive gift in itself.

We lived on the Essex/Suffolk border, roughly 50 miles away from the Big Smoke and a day like this did not come around that often. Also, I was aware that it was to be the last big Gribble outing as a foursome before another brother or sister was added to the fold so I was determined to have a really good time.

We walked along Tower Bridge as the bright lights glistened in the December sky, and yet all I could think of was a row of Daleks marauding towards me. We stopped and stared at the shop windows along Regent Street and my mind's eye made those shop window dummies come to life, smashing their way through the plate glass and advancing on me with guns protruding. I couldn't even look at a manhole cover without imagining a Cyberman punching it sky high and an army of the silver giants marching down the steps of St Paul's.

Most of these visions were coming to me courtesy of a video I'd purchased back home called *More Than Thirty Years in the TARDIS*. A couple of months previously, I'd plucked up the courage to enter a second-hand shop called *Record Peddler* in town on my own whilst my parents were nearby and found that glorious love letter to the show in a dark corner of the shop. The man who owned it and sold the said video tape to me went on to win £148 million on the National Lottery in 2011.

The front cover was splendid. It showed the TARDIS in what looked like the innards of a Rubik's Cube and, on the back, promised interviews, behind-the-scenes footage and clips galore of the show that had almost become my life. Happily, it more than lived up to its promise. I played it over and over again that winter. How I laughed when I heard Jon Pertwee say that there was nothing more alarming than seeing a Yeti on your loo in Tooting Bec. I was delighted to see cine film footage of William Hartnell waving from the back of a jeep (I wondered at the time if it was a UNIT vehicle and the Brigadier was at the wheel).

CHILD OUT OF TIME

It was fantastic to see Frazer Hines and Deborah Watling together on the set of *The Evil of the Daleks* talking about the best Doctor of them all, Patrick Troughton, and lamenting the fact that some of their best work had been confined to the great junkyard in the sky. The only disappointment for me was that two Doctors were missing from the extravaganza. Tom Baker and Peter Davison were nowhere to be seen but it was great to see that Gerry Anderson (the god of all things *Supermarionation*) had a son who looked roughly my age and was perched on an armchair professing his love for *Doctor Who*, despite the fact that his own father appeared slighted. After all, he was the one who gave us *Thunderbirds* and *Captain Scarlet*!

The tape was yet another gem to add to my growing collection. And its dream-like sequences of the little boy being chased by a gallery of the Doctor's best enemies was filling my imagination as I walked the crisp, cold streets of London.

After a while, my family and I were examining the many extortionate trinkets in Harrods when, in their entertainment section, something caught my eye. It called out to me from the bargain bin in the centre of the aisle, placed carefully to entice those already queuing with their purchases. I delved in and fished out a *Doctor Who* video. And this one was to form a special place in my affections for the show.

It was *Pyramids of Mars*, one of the Doctor Who stories I had been pining to see. The front cover showed the Fourth Doctor leaning against a dark and menacing sarcophagus and at the foot of the image was a cream pyramid that looked like it was being closely guarded by mummies. In those days, I was an avid admirer of the Egyptians and longed to visit King Tutankhamun's tomb and the Sphinx.

Harrods was the last place I expected to find anything to do with *Doctor Who*, let alone an adventure that I'd long wanted to see. It wasn't like today where you could go anywhere in the world and find anything from a *Character Options* action figure of an Axon or slippers with David Tennant's face on them. I feverishly checked my pockets for the remnants of the cash that Mum and Dad had allowed me to spend on our day out. I knew that videos were pretty expensive. I once spent £34.99 on the E-Space trilogy box set and had next to no birthday money left. And I don't even like *Warriors Gate* that much! So, I prayed I would have enough. Luckily, Harrods high cost stock did not extend to its bargain bin and the £9.99 would easily be covered by the manky looking ten pound note that had started to congeal in my pocket.

When we got home that evening, I asked my parents if I could watch a bit of the story before bed time. Happily, after some coercing, they relented. As the dark night drew in even further, I popped that cassette in and was instantly transported to 1975. As I watched that brilliant first episode, something washed over me. Something that I'd never experienced before as a *Doctor Who* fan but which generations of children have felt before or since when peering into the Doctor's universe. As the situation grew graver and as Sutekh the Destroyer's pawns moved in a chess game that the Doctor looked increasingly likely to lose, I started to feel scared.

This time, it didn't look like the Doctor and Sarah would be able to save the day. I had witnessed Namin burn to his death at the hands of a possessed Marcus Scarman and then, most terrifying of all, I'd been whisked away along with Sarah and Marcus's terrified brother, Lawrence, to a nightmare vision of 1980. And then, just to make things worse, a being as malevolent and powerful as Sutekh could hurt the Doctor with just the power of his mind. He turned my hero in Sutekh's plaything, told him he was nothing but an insect and that he could shred his nervous system into a million fibres and keep him alive in agony for the rest of eternity. Not even the Daleks had the power to do that! At ten years old, this genuinely unsettled me.

In all my previous Doctor Who binges, there was never a shred of doubt that the Doctor was going to win and that good would triumph. But this time, especially when he was possessed by a being so truly terrifying, I had no idea how it was going to end. But I knew that I wanted the Doctor and Sarah to be okay so that I could feel safe watching them again. And yet, despite my anxieties over the story and where the resolution was going, I loved it. It became my new favourite story and, to this day, shares that honour with *The Web of Fear* as my favourite *Doctor Who* story of all time. I wonder if the fact that I watched it at night had anything to do with my terror back in December 1999.

However, the genius of *Pyramids of Mars* was not the only new 'old' *Who* I was to discover that winter. In all my discoveries, this one was to bamboozle me even more than the revelation that the Doctor was an alien who could change his face or the concept of a time travelling police box. It was even more bizarre than the impending bundle of joy that was to join my little family. This mystery wrapped in Christmas paper was in the form of another video cassette. And it bore the face of a Doctor I'd never seen or even heard of before. What's more, I recognised the face. It was that of Grand Moff Tarkin, the man who gave the order to destroy Alderaan in *Star Wars*. It was Peter Cushing as the Doctor. In my hands, was *Doctor Who and the Daleks*. And it was a total anomaly.

I recall, when looking through the pages of the *Radio Times* 1996 pull-out, seeing a tiny, postage stamp poster for a movie bearing that title. But this glimmer of information was swamped by everything else in that fantastic magazine. Somehow, my uncle had heard of my love for *Doctor Who*, and managed to dig this out from somewhere. At the time, I thought he may have discovered it in a parallel dimension where my favourite programme was not a TV show but a multi-million movie franchise like the aforementioned *Star Wars*. And, if he had slipped sideways into another version of our world, then naturally I wanted to know how!

In the end, much to my disappointment, this parallel world turned out to be Woolworths. But this new film was to add another facet of wonder to my little universe. It was *Doctor Who*...but not as I knew it.

For starters, it appeared that 'Doctor Who' was the Time Lord's real name. And not only that, but he didn't appear to have the same origins as his TV namesake. There was no mention of Gallifrey or the Doctor's heritage. He was an inventor and a grandfather to Susan (who appeared in the guise of a ten-year-old girl) and Barbara (who was much younger and more alluring than Jacqueline Hill to me). And, to round off this strange iteration, Ian Chesterton was now played by the bloke from *Record Breakers*!

There was no console within the TARDIS, just a myriad of wires and dials in what looked like a shed painted in cream. It lacked the sleek splendour of the one I'd grown to love.

Yet there was so much to love about the movie. The score was so expansive. The Dalek city and the depiction of the Thals were just as I'd imagined in my dreams. Skaro had never looked so good. The Dalek city was brimming with gleaming metal and the kind of futuristic imagery that I saw when I closed my eyes. To juxtapose its beauty, the petrified forest that the Thals were doomed to dwell in was just as tormented and devastated as I'd always wanted it to be. And to top it off, these colourful machines were so superior to the ones I'd been watching on those faded VHS tapes. They even killed with a deadly shot of fire extinguisher foam – how cool is that!

Before long, I had given in to the charm of the sequel, *Dalek Invasion of Earth: 2150 AD* too. If anything, it was even better than its predecessor. My verdict was improved by the addition of Sir Bernard of Cribbins as Tom the Policeman at the expense of the hapless Roy Castle. He was stronger, braver and above all funnier, especially in the scene when he imitated the emotionless Robomen in the flying saucer. He had clearly read the manual of how to be a companion as he correctly referred to the Doctor as 'the Doctor' - there was none of this 'Doctor Who' rubbish.

I was still perplexed as to why Susan had this terrible habit of twisting her ankle in moments of mild peril but the action-packed fun ride was just what the Doctor ordered and a stark improvement on its televisual counterpart. I had awful recollections of what I perceived as a cheap, black and white telling of the same tale. This story was more concise and the setting more expansive. It really did look like London had been devastated by a Dalek invasion and the mutated monsters were victorious. But there was still one problem with these films that I couldn't get over. This Doctor just wasn't the Doctor.

Peter Cushing was a worthy hero but, in my opinion, he was no William Hartnell....or Patrick Troughton. Heck, he wasn't even Rowan Atkinson! So, although I thoroughly enjoyed both of his adventures and encounters with the Daleks, there was too little of the Doctor in Cushing's performances in both films. But there was more to come as my hobby was becoming gluttony.

Not long after *Doctor Who Night*, the next day in fact, the BBC had begun a short lived yet pants-wetting, exciting repeat run of the Jon Pertwee era. It all began with a double bill of his debut story, *Spearhead from Space*, a story that my cousin, Mike, had purchased on video but that I wanted for myself. So there I was, 6pm on the dot, sitting with anticipation by the television, my finger hovering over the record button on my parents' VCR.

I hoped that this repeat run, in the same broadcasting slot as the monstrously popular American sitcom, *The Simpsons*, would peak an interest in the show among my friends. Earlier in the year, my Show and Tell had ignited a spark with my peers but, when they actually saw what the best special effects thirty year-old science fiction had to offer, the flame was never lit.

Still, it was heaven to watch *Doctor Who* in episodic form for the first time. My affection for the Third Doctor, helped by the fact that he had been my mum's favourite, meant that, for the first time in my life, every week I was waiting with glee for the latest instalment. And even though I knew the general gist of what was going to happen in the upcoming episodes, I was at last going to watch them with my own eyes. It also meant that I could tick them off one by one in the availability checklist in the back of my already battered copy of *Doctor Who: The Television Companion*.

However, the wonders of modern technology didn't always guarantee a recording on that old VCR. Around the time that a double bill of Episodes 2 and 3 of *Doctor Who and the Silurians* was about to air, we discovered that our VCR was failing to pick up the picture, only the audio on a blank, hazy screen. My dad tried to remedy this by jamming the SCART lead further into its housing in the back of the TV but it was no use.

CHILD OUT OF TIME

Also, the VCR occasionally slipped its timer record function, decided to forego the channel we'd selected and recorded something entirely different. *Heartbeat* springs to mind as one of those taped to our surprise on a boring Sunday night.

As Christmas was upon us and panto season was well underway, I was dragged kicking and screaming to my Reception class's performance of Pinocchio. On that very same night, two episodes of *The Silurians* were airing and our video recorder was acting temperamental. It was torture sitting through that play, crossing my fingers so tightly for the video to be recording that my eyes were watering. My dad thought I was stoked by Clara's fantastic portrayal as the pivotal Villager 1! Thankfully, on this occasion, technology and luck were on my side and both Episodes 2 and 3 were captured for eternity. We eventually binned that untrustworthy VCR and purchased a new one in between the final part of *The Silurians* and Episode 1 of *Genesis of the Daleks*. This was another story I'd longed to see, partly because it was Davros's first but mainly because I'd developed a real love for the Fourth Doctor, Sarah and Harry. I loved *Genesis*. Not as much as *Pyramids*, mind, but, for five weeks (as there was another double bill in the story), I was gripped by Terry Nation's gritty tale of the birth of the greatest monsters ever to take on the Doctor. I found it curious, however, why the BBC had decided to jump straight from *The Silurians* to *Genesis* and, for a brief moment, sweated over the notion that the Beeb had only gone and destroyed more episodes! I must have missed the copy of *DWM* that explained the gap and the eventual end of repeats.

That run of repeats might have been short but it was needed. *Doctor Who* was still a major point of interest in my life. I'd even started to craft my own video front covers so that these domestic recordings of *Spearhead*, *Silurians* and *Genesis* could sit on the video shelf next to their BBC endorsed counterparts and not feel left out. There was many an old copy of *DWM* that disappeared by way of scissors and Sellotape to provide my art.

Something that had been a love and a passion was starting to become a distraction from bigger world events. I began watching, reading and writing more about the Doctor to make me forget the changes that were about to occur. With the oncoming sibling and the impending move to secondary school, it felt like my whole life was about to enter a whole new and scary era.

But, before all of that, there was one more thing to come which would truly expose me as a massive *Doctor Who* fan. And for once, I would be surrounded by like-minded people who loved the show almost as much as I did.

Around the time that my sister and I had been told that a baby brother or sister was on its way, we went for our almost monthly visit to Clacton to see

Nan and Grandad. I always got excited about seeing my grandparents and the tantalising promise of visiting that book shop on Kings Avenue and purchasing a tatty old Target novelisation. But, on this occasion, they had something extra special planned for me.

Instead of taking that long, familiar walk to the sea front, Dad ushered the pair of us into the family Vauxhall. He was unusually quiet, like someone who had got a secret up his sleeve. His manner reminded me of Captain Scarlet not long after he's taken over by the Mysterons. Happily, instead of driving off to a London Car-Vu where we'd come under attack from a helicopter, he drove us to a little seaside town not far away called Frinton. Looking back now, I think that Dad was playing a little trick on us. As one former Doctor Who producer once put it, the memory cheats as it was actually Clacton we stayed in.

I thought this even stranger than before. Why had we gone to Frinton? I remember Nan telling me that she had seen Roger Moore sunbathing there with his father many years ago and wondered if I was off to meet the great 007 himself. When we reached our destination, I wasn't ludicrously wide of the mark!

We parked up and proceeded on foot to what looked like an old church hall. I thought I was in some weird version of Neverland. Mingling outside was a group of people dressed in rough approximations of costumes from *Star Trek*, *Star*

Wars, *Babylon 5* and, to my utter astonishment, *Doctor Who*! I yelped at the sight! I was about to attend my first Science Fiction convention.

As I recall, it was a surreal and at times disconcerting experience. For one thing, I don't remember many children there. In the main hall, there was a wide range of stalls full of tempting merchandise, but my dad wasn't willing to part with his hard-earned money for what he called 'extortionate' prices for all manner of trinkets. And there wasn't really anything that stood out to me at the time as a must have buy.

The biggest attraction of the day was, of course, the stars on the guest list who were sitting like gods on the stage at the far end of the hall. I had no idea that stars of the big and small screen would be there to sign autographs for the eager fans queuing to meet their heroes. I was totally blown away when I recognised some, including Bond girl Caroline Munro, *Star Wars* legends Peter Mayhew (Chewbacca) and Kenny Baker (R2-D2) and will never forget the look on my dad's face when he spoke to Peter. He was having a fan boy moment, make no mistake!

Unfortunately, he then made me cringe so hard that I scrunched my eyelids together until I saw nothing but white dots for a few moments. When we arrived at the table of Femi Taylor who played the ill-fated dancer Oola, who fell to the Rancor after displeasing the villainous Jabba the Hutt in

Return of the Jedi, my father decided to use his charm and wit on the poor unsuspecting actress. 'Oh,' he chirped. 'So, you're not really green in real life, then!'

I'm pretty sure the term 'face palm' hadn't been invented yet but, my god, it was what was needed in this embarrassing moment! Luckily, Taylor was utterly delightful in response to a truly terrible chat up line and laughed to put us at our ease us and signed the convention programme I thrust in front of her.

After that ordeal, we came upon two stars that I knew very well. Sitting together were two people who were synonymous with my favourite Doctor, Patrick Troughton. I identified them immediately and instantly twigged why Dad had brought me to this utterly mad event. In front of me were Victoria Waterfield and Professor Travers themselves, the brilliant Deborah and Jack Watling.

I felt a warm glow of happiness run over me and my face burned above my fixed smile at seeing two such prestigious people in my fandom. Deborah Watling was one of the women who adorned my Geography book back at school. Alongside Princess Leia and Minnie the Minx, she was the only female representative in a collage of comic book characters, cartoons and space heroes. And now here she was in the flesh, sitting just a few feet away from me.

I was startled to see just how little she and her father had aged in the intervening three decades since they appeared in Doctor Who. I wasn't entirely sure what to say to them, except that I was a massive fan, a customary statement at any convention. She then asked me who my favourite Doctor was. I told her that Troughton and Tom Baker were the best in my view, something that visibly pleased her as she beamed back at me. Deborah then asked me which stories were my favourite. Around that time, I was rather obsessed with the Ice Warriors (possibly influenced by obtaining their debut story in a box-set a year before) and, of course, *The Web of Fear*. I confessed to her that my Target novelisation of *Web* had been pinched from my school library. I suddenly felt like a child in the dock, spilling out a dark secret that I was soon to be punished for. Not even Dad knew about my tendency to steal books from school!

I will love Deborah Watling forever for what she said next. She beckoned me forward and leant over the table to whisper in my ear.
'Have you written your name in it?' she enquired.
'Yes,' I lied.
'Well, it's yours now, and don't let anyone else tell you otherwise.'

I smiled a smile that would brighten the darkest days. She then signed the programme as did her father, who didn't speak at all, and we left their presence to browse the stalls once again, pausing briefly in front of a Dalek prop for a photograph I insisted my Dad take.

Later on that day, we bumped into the Watlings again as they were shopping in Clacton. I bounded over to them, not thinking through what I was going to say and, beaming like an idiot as my embarrassed father watched on. I ran up to them, yelled hello, which they returned, and then I realised I had nothing else to say and ran away again. I have no idea why I did that, but to stand among those I considered giants, even for a brief second, was the stuff of dreams. However, the convention bug failed to bite me. I was unmoved by the cosplayers, alienated by the lack of my peers at the event and horrified at the expensive merchandise on display. It would be a long time before I ventured to a similar event again. But I'd never forget that day or Dad for taking me.

March 18th 2000 was a red letter day in the Gribble household. It was the day that my youngest sister was born. It was a crisp spring morning and my life was to change in a year that was all about new beginnings and challenges. Unlike many of my school friends, who spoke of their dread and jealousy when their mum and dad informed them of their impending little bundle of joy, I wasn't threatened. On the contrary, I was already planning to brainwash him (I was praying extra hard that it was going to be a brother) into my multi-coloured world of science fiction and action bliss. I even had a fantastic plan to get this soon-to-be sibling to play *Star Wars* with me. She would be devastated to learn later on in life that I fully intended to carry her around in a backpack whilst attempting back flips!

Sadly, my predictions of a boy were thwarted as I was now the only son in a five-person family. I knew that I was outnumbered as soon as I heard Rohanna's first cry through the crack in the door of our living room.

As this new baby took away some of the attention previously awarded to Clara and I, we both had to adjust to this very small person in our lives. We reaped benefits in other, more material ways. One of the biggest bonuses of the arrival of a new sibling is the enormous glut of presents that are bestowed upon you. As your parents, grandparents, aunts, uncles and well-wishers spend their time showing affection to this new imposter to your cosy world, you often find yourself well compensated in return. And this is exactly what happened to my sister and me.

Among the gifts was a brand new *Doctor Who* VHS. Whilst my sister received a tape of *Barbie and the Nutcracker*, I was rewarded with *The Invasion of Time*. Initially, I was over the moon to add another piece to my puzzle but, after watching all six episodes in one go, something peculiar happened to me. It was the first time I was totally underwhelmed by a *Doctor Who* story. My perception filter had well and truly broken and the illusion was shattered forever. To my ageing, suddenly cynical eyes, my favourite programme looked cheap and old.

I was dismayed by the flimsy Vardans whose kitchen foil appearance defied any suspension of disbelief. I was shocked at an unlikeable performance from the always-reliable Fourth Doctor. The politics and bureaucracy of the Time Lords made me yawn so hard that I lost all interest. Not even the presence of the lovely Leela and K-9 could keep my attention. With a baby in the room, and SATS exams to prepare for, *The Invasion of Time* was a catalyst to the ending of my love affair with Doctor Who. Over the next couple of months, I stopped reaching for my videos, leafing through my Target books and instead I began to feel the new responsibility of being not only a big brother to two little sisters but the pressure of getting good grades that would determine my placement in certain subjects at secondary school.

Maybe if that video had been something classic and enthralling like *Earthshock* or *The Talons of Weng-Chiang,* then I wouldn't have lost interest in my favourite programme. And yet, within a couple of years, the pictures on my wall had melted away from *DWM* cut outs and were now replaced with images of my favourite footballers and Holly Valance. The videos and books were pushed further to the outer reaches of my shelves and became covered in thick layers of dust and my handwritten stories were filed away or binned, never to see daylight again. Just four years after discovering the greatest and most important TV show of all time, I had fallen out of love with *Doctor Who*…seemingly for good.

CHAPTER NINE
REGENERATION

It will forever be one of the first questions that fans of a certain generation will turn to each other and ask themselves. Where were you when you heard the news that Doctor Who was coming back?

For years, I couldn't for the life of me recall my location when I saw the announcement on that weekday in September 2003, but recently I was a guest on a well-regarded podcast where the host asked me that very question. And all of a sudden, it came flooding back to me.

In fact, the question triggered such a vivid recollection of my whereabouts that I can picture it now. I was sitting in the media room at my school, browsing away whilst doing my best to look like I was really getting on with my homework. You see, our school scolded us for the misuse of its IT equipment. We were ever so innocent back then, and the naughtiest thing we had ever googled was the game sites *Miniclip* and *Stick Cricket*. Patrolling teachers would regularly look over my shoulder and scare me witless with a remark along the lines of 'I don't think BBC Sport has anything to do with osmosis in potatoes, does it, Hayden?' Some would still debate the merits of whether it does.

Yet on this occasion, I was lucky. It was lunchtime and a friend and I had sneaked into the media room after trying the door handle and finding the room unlocked. It was a dark and dingy little bunker situated next to our main hall, where we would assemble for meetings and at lunchtimes our delightful school dinners would be dispensed. There were several machines on the work benches with wires jutting out of every available plug and wall crevice.

We assumed our positions at those PCs we knew were the fastest and most reliable and opened up our work, which we could pull up over Internet Explorer just in case we were discovered. I typed the URL for the BBC Website, scrolled down the page and noticed a picture of Tom Baker and Lalla Ward with a Dalek and the tagline 'DOCTOR WHO RETURNS TO TV'.

It had been a long time in my young life since the show made a massive impact on me. I was different now and felt like I'd left *Doctor Who* behind. Secondary school had changed me. I was not the floppy haired, bouncy boy I once was. Now, I was all spiky hair, punk and nu metal music and zits. My experiences over the last few years had jaded my opinion of education and deep down I wanted to escape the trappings of the prison I felt I was in. You'd have thought that an appointment with the returning Doctor was just what I needed.

Except as I read the article, I felt no wonderful rush of excitement. I had moved on from *Doctor Who*. I was 14 and my life was all about football, cricket and girls now. My three main areas of interest didn't really allow much room for something that I thought would be laughed at by my school chums. It's my belief to this day that no one is really themselves during their senior years in education. Life in those concrete walls is all about conformity and going along with the crowd. If you deviate from it, you're an outcast. Life and people are so fickle at that age and I had changed so much to fit in. I wasn't even writing or drawing like I used to and if I did, those sketches and scribbles were quickly pushed under my bed whenever my friends came over. Individuality and creativity were almost scowled upon by the guys I hung out with back then. At least that's how I felt. Looking back, these were truly my missing years in more ways than one.

Deep down, there was a mild curiosity as to how the new show would pan out and I knew I would probably peek in just to see what it was like. But would it appeal to me? After all, even though my generation had been deprived so badly of the show, I had been raised watching the classics of yesteryear. Would this even be a continuation of the show or just a reboot? I wasn't sure how I would feel if I heard that the show which had been there so many times for me in the past was now redundant and defunct.

I scoured the article for clues as to what the future had in store for the series. A man called Russell T Davies was to be the show runner. I'd heard of him before as in the late 1990s his name appeared frequently in issues of *DWM* plugging his TV show, *Queer as Folk* (whatever that was, as I wasn't allowed up very late to watch it) and discussing what he would do with the show if it were to be brought back for a millennial audience. And now it was happening. I liked his enthusiasm and wished that I could match it.

'*Doctor Who* is one of the BBC's most exciting and original characters. He's had a good rest and now it's time to bring him back!' he exclaimed whilst Julie Gardner (Head of Drama at BBC Wales), who would be making the programme, tempered his excitement with 'this is very early days and it is unlikely anything will be on screen for at least two years but it is very exciting and I can't wait to get started.'

Two years! That's how long it was going to take to get it on TV? And why BBC Wales? If the BBC really were serious about making the show as great as it once was, wouldn't it be made at the lovely old Television Centre in London? I was filled with trepidation at all this news.

The news hadn't escaped the attention of my parents either. After another perilous bus journey through the narrow rural roads that wound their way from school to my village, my mum broke away from her cooking and blurted the news out as soon as I'd set foot into our hallway. She seemed positively effervescent. How I envied her!

I wanted to feel excited about it. I really did. Besides, maybe *Doctor Who* wasn't as niche and silly as I assumed other people considered it. One of the biggest shows we would watch at that age was *Dead Ringers* and one of the segments that would get spoken about at school the next day was John Culshaw's flawless impersonation of the great Tom Baker. But his hilarious sketches just continued to hammer it home to me that the show was dead. I certainly thought it was.

I've spoken to many people since then who've assured me that, deep down, they'd always expected the show to return one day. But these friends were all older than me and had watched the show when they were kids in the Seventies and Eighties. It was never there for me on TV, barring repeats and, of course, my well-worn VHS collection. So, it had always seemed to be in the past for me.

Also, when you are a teenager, nostalgia doesn't interest you, only what's current. You try so hard to grow up and, in the process, do your utmost to leave behind what you used to be like and what interests you had. Essentially, you try to shed that skin and grow a new, mature one to impress others. But in doing so, you forget what made you what you were in the first place. That's what I was doing at the time. Happily, as you get older, you learn to embrace all the different people you've been throughout your life and realise that your personality is made up of who you have been up until now. If anything, I have more in common now with my ten-year-old-self than I have with that rather shallow and superficial teen. Who'd have thought that growing up would mean not growing up at all?

However, after a delayed reaction, I did start to feel a warm glow that my once-favourite show was coming back. As media rumblings began to predict the identity of the new Doctor, I too started to wonder who might pick up the TARDIS keys and make that blue box fly again. A lot of the papers were suggesting actors who to me weren't really actors. Comedians like Eddie Izzard and Alan Davies were seemingly linked for months but, for me, the role needed someone with dramatic gravitas. Someone who could grab the Daleks by the baubles and make them shudder with fear.

I remember picking up a newspaper and seeing that an actor by the name of Christopher Eccleston had won the part. I'd recently seen him star alongside Nicholas Cage in *Gone in Sixty Seconds* on the school coach coming back from a trip and had really liked him. There was something about his seriousness in the film that finally convinced me that this revival of *Doctor Who* might be successful after all. It needed a strong leading man to convince me that this new show might just have what it took to make it big. And I hadn't even seen any footage of him yet.

Within the next two years, that nostalgia would begin to bleed through. In late 2003, there were three events that helped my love for the show bloom again, albeit slowly. The first, rather sadly, passed me by. It was a brand new episode of *Doctor Who* streamed on the BBC website called *Scream of the Shalka*. I remember flicking through a *Sci-Fi Now* magazine which looked into the story in depth but I knew very little about it except that Richard E Grant played a rather cantankerous and angry version of the Ninth Doctor and that it was an animation from the company that made *Count Duckula* and *Dangermouse* (the now sadly defunct Cosgrove Hall Productions).

As we were still cursed with a dial-up modem at home, which took the same amount of time to load a single image that it takes to fry an egg on a cold stove, I tried accessing *Shalka* at school. However, the internet police caught me one lunchtime as I tried to watch it in a pop-up window on the desktop and I promptly gave up pursuing it. In fact, to this day, I still haven't seen it.

Even though I was deep in the turmoil of adolescence, I still watched *Blue Peter* on the pretext that I had two little sisters who enjoyed it, even if I was growing out of it. However, I sat down one Friday in November, around the time of *Doctor Who*'s 40th Anniversary, and to my shock and delight, found it full of *Who* nostalgia. The highlight for me was a *Who*-themed quiz between the Seventh Doctor himself, Sylvester McCoy, and a young fan. I envied this fan slightly because years earlier, I had wanted to be on *Blue Peter*. Not even my three *Blue Peter* badges awarded for drawings when I used to watch the show avidly could soothe my disappointment. I can't for the life of me remember who won but I have a feeling it was the Time Lord.

And then, there was *The Story of Doctor Who*, a documentary covering the show's 40-year history. In my opinion, it lacked the magic of *More Than Thirty Years in the TARDIS* but it was an admirable update with such glorious talking heads as the Doctors themselves; Tom Baker, Peter Davison, Colin Baker and Sylvester McCoy. They were also joined by luminaries like Verity Lambert, Peter Purves, Frazer Hines, Elisabeth Sladen, Nicholas Courtney and Sophie Aldred. It was great to see the old clips again, including ones from stories I still hadn't seen up to this point, but the positivity coming from the contributors was easy to pick up on. It seemed to me that the good feeling towards the programme was ebbing back following the news of the show's impending return. And it was a feeling that had started to work its magic on me.

I began thinking about the impact this new incarnation would have on my three-year-old sister. She would be five when *Doctor Who* returned. The perfect age, some would say, to start her adventures with the good Doctor. I was already anticipating how many of my school chums could be persuaded to watch the show. I also began to ask whether old school fans would even like it and, more importantly, would I? Time would have to tell. It always does.

As more and more news started to seep out of BBC Wales, I was absolutely floored by the announcement of the lucky actress who'd been cast to play the Doctor's new companion. Who would be Christopher Eccleston's brand new best friend, following in the footsteps of such brilliant assistants as Katy Manning, Elisabeth Sladen, Janet Fielding and Sophie Aldred? Someone who could hold their own in an alien world, ask all the questions the fans are screaming at the TV screen, twist their ankle in a small divot in the ground to render themselves incapacitated or captured and generally get themselves into trouble so the Doctor could lead a heroic rescue attempt. Also, I always found myself slightly attracted to most of the female companions that I'd seen on old tapes.

And, above all, I wanted someone who was a well-known actress.

When I heard the new companion was going to be played by Billie Piper, I nearly fell off my stool in the chemistry room at school!

It had all been going so well. It had all looked so positive and lovely. I couldn't imagine why someone I perceived as a pop star had won the role. Could it really be that the same girl who had plagued my ear drums back in primary school with such terrible 'hits' as *Because We Want To* and *Honey to the Bee* was now going to be a part of the greatest television programme ever made? I thought back to all the various accounts I'd read of the show's downfall, when producer John Nathan Turner began recruiting the likes of Ken Dodd, Beryl Reid and Hale and Pace to star in the programme. The light entertainment aspect of these casting decisions only served to speed up the downward spiral that *Doctor Who* was in by the mid-to-late Eighties and here it was happening again. In truth, I despaired.

Then I caught a TV dramatisation of *The Canterbury Tales* and, to my shock, Billie Piper was one of the main cast. 'Well, this is just the BBC putting her in anything they can to prove to doubters like me that she'll be very good,' I hypothesised, but actually, she was rather good as Alison Crosby alongside James Nesbitt and Dennis Waterman in an episode called *The*

Miller's Tale. I started thinking that maybe my disappointment and bemusement at her winning the role as the Doctor's companion was misplaced. I then discovered that she had in fact been training to become an actress when she was snapped up by the music business. Maybe, just maybe, she would turn out alright. And so, with just over 18 months to go before the first episode of *Doctor Who* in nearly a decade, I got on with my life and awaited the Doctor's return.

March 2005

It had been a long, long, impatient wait. In the time that had elapsed, I had continued my studies at secondary school and was now gearing up for the most important exams in my short life; the dreaded GCSEs. Eleven timed examinations that tested my mental capability in an array of academic subjects. Around February, some of my classmates had already started the monotonous practice of revision and the unforgiving deadlines of coursework had surged towards me in a tidal wave of paper and red marker. I still had my problems at school. Nothing had really changed in the last couple of years and if anything, the impending doom of exams had increased my anxieties. I was working below many of my target grades and had seriously fallen behind in the subject that had once been my saving grace; English. In a top-set-class where I was expected to obtain a double A grade for Language and Literature, I was working at a D. But by the early Spring of 2005, only one D was on my mind, and his name was the Doctor.

I had deliberately avoided the tantalising copies of *DWM* and various other science fiction magazines in the newsagents and did little else on the internet than converse with my friends on MSN chat rooms and look up Franz Ferdinand gig tickets that I could not afford, so there was still very little I knew about this new series. The concept of a fan forum was as alien to me back then as the complexities of a chameleon circuit so I had done very well to avoid anything that would spoil the surprise of what this new *Doctor Who* would be like.

And then one day, I could avoid it no longer. In early March, we were making a family trip to London when, all of a sudden, I was startled to see a billboard carrying a photograph of Christopher Eccleston and Billie Piper, gazing off into the far distance with a look of determination and fun in their eyes as light shone gloriously out of the open doors of the TARDIS, that brilliant blue box that was still the object of my dreams. And in white block writing, the words I had longed to see since that May evening in the Midlands back in 1996 shot out from the poster:

CHILD OUT OF TIME

DOCTOR WHO
SATURDAYS 7PM
BBC ONE

It was back…and it was about time!

From here on in, I would do all I could to find any crumb of information about the new show. My mother bought the *Radio Times* (the cornerstone of British TV news, I thought) every week and then, one glorious day, I picked up the latest copy from the magazine rack in our living room and gazed in wonder at a police box on the front cover. Finally, this was all starting to feel so real.

What still stands out for me now from that memorable issue was the centrefold souvenir and that first glimpse of the new TARDIS console. It was then that I realised absolutely everything about this new incarnation of the show was going to be brilliant. The new console looked as though it had grown organically, standing proud with its central column reaching high. I had never for one minute believed that the bright, white cleanliness of the console room that the 1980s Doctors had used was going to return but to see the TARDIS so vast and so alive warmed my heart.

I was ever so slightly disappointed, however, to finally see the new Doctor's costume for the first time. There were no frills, no frock coat, no long scarf or question marks on his shirt collar. This Doctor wore a battered leather jacket, black trousers, a jumper and a haircut cropped so short it made him look like a skinhead. This new look was so unconventional, so different to anything that had gone before. And yet, it looked brilliant.

It wasn't just the pictures that drew me in. There were wonderful sneak peeks at what this new 13-part series was going to include. Autons, a trip to the day the Earth died in a ball of flames, gas mask zombies and, most tantalizingly of all, the last Dalek in existence. I wanted to know everything!

Eccleston's Doctor was going to blow me away, I was sure, and my mum had already taken a liking to this new incarnation. Being a product of the Jon Pertwee era, I never thought she could possibly take another Doctor for her own. Despite this, as soon as we watched the first trailer, with the Ninth Doctor looking up at the viewer and asking 'Do you want to come with me?' in his broad Northern accent, she was in love with a new Doctor. And, in a different way, so was I.

The excitement was palpable in my household in the week leading up to the first episode of 21st century *Who* - the wonderfully and evocatively titled *Rose*. We watched everything. The BBC News spots and the trailers including that fantastic fireball footage that sadly was never included in the actual series. We even caught a thought provoking edition of *The Culture Show* in which presenter Matthew Sweet bemoaned the notion that *Doctor Who* might now cease its life as a cult, personal addiction for fans and pondered its future as a mainstream success and how it couldn't be both. The VCR worked overtime that week, capturing absolutely everything to do with *Doctor Who* that crossed the five channels we had at our disposal.

We plonked my youngest sister down in front of the TV for that Friday's edition of *Blue Peter* in a desperate attempt to brainwash her into liking *Doctor Who*. She hadn't had the exposure my middle sister had as a child, although even she hadn't really like any of the stories I used to force her to watch with me unless Patrick Troughton or Sylvester McCoy were in them. So, she'd missed out on my fanatical days as a young fan. She sat there, gaping at Christopher Eccleston as he made a humble yet mildly embarrassed appearance on the flagship children's show and she was utterly besotted by the monsters that that she saw, especially these new, green adversaries that we would later find out were named the Slitheen.

'So, will you be watching with me tomorrow?' I asked her.

'If I'm allowed,' she replied sweetly.

That evening also saw the tireless Eccleston making an appearance on *The Jonathan Ross Show* which I had managed to pick up on my knackered 15" TV that possessed a wonky aerial and had a tendency to fade into a snowstorm every five seconds. I picked up on a slightly negative vibe from my new hero. He kept talking about how he had filmed two series back to back as the episodes run times were double that of the original series (which, thanks to that trusty old *Doctor Who Yearbook*, I knew was a load of rubbish) and I recall that he bemoaned the fact that he had to shave every day for the last nine months and how he had done nothing else in that time. I wasn't completely taken with his tone. In a way, it sounded like he'd already had enough of the role and we hadn't even seen him yet! Surely he wouldn't last just one series if the show was a resounding success?

I recall little of what else happened on the day of March 26th 2005. I can't remember what I did during the day or who I spent it with. But I will never forget the feeling of excitement as I sat on that old sofa, full of anticipation, my fingers crossed and my heart pounding as the Doctor flew back onto our TV screens.

Before the main attraction, there was a short documentary called *Doctor Who: A New Dimension*, which served as an appetiser to fans of old and a hook to pull the new, younger audience towards the show that evening. It was that first time that any *Who* fan had heard a snippet of the new theme tune, unless they'd downloaded the leaked copy of *Rose* which had been extradited from a Canadian broadcaster, I learnt years later. Again, it hadn't occurred to me that Delia Derbyshire's wonderful arrangement would be updated for the umpteenth time, but the string arrangement that accompanied what was clearly a sample taken from the original score was like balm for my ears.

The following thirty minutes was a brilliant reintroduction of the Doctor for the millennial generation. Clips of the previous incarnations of the Doctor were partnered with the music of the time, evoking enough nostalgia to keep the parents happy but engaging the children enough to keep them occupied with what was happening on the screen. What I liked about this retrospective was the way in which the new head writer, Russell T Davies, waxed lyrical about each and every actor to play the Time Lord. In the past, I'd fallen out of love with the likes of the First, Sixth and Seventh Doctors, but seeing their best moments incorporated with the new man in charge of the show made me re-evaluate their credentials.

What was most exciting about this documentary was that it gave fleeting glimpses into adventures that were coming up soon. I drooled with anticipation at the sight of a murderous Dalek on the rampage in what looked like a military base. The ominous vision of dozens of advancing gas mask zombies and an animated corpse swathed in blue light whet my pallet for what would be an incredible 13 weeks.

Narrated by some Scottish actor called David Tennant (I only knew him from a BBC Three show called *Casanova*, which I may have peeped into as I had heard there may be some scenes of an adult nature – I was fifteen after all!) and including more sound bites from the likes of Eccleston, Piper, Davies and Mark Gatiss (who was writing the hotly anticipated third episode), it was *Who* heaven.

All of a sudden, I was that seven-year-old again, sitting in the old folks' home in Warwickshire, poring over every minute detail of that *Radio Times* pull-out. I was excited and curious again and the hour that separated the documentary from the main event felt like forever. It didn't help that there was a live clock ticking down throughout *A New Dimension*, heralding the Doctor's long overdue return.

And then, for the first time I can remember, all five of us, Mum, Dad, my two sisters and I, were all perched on the sofa, waiting for the moment that I had been counting down for the previous two years. This was it. The first time that *Doctor Who* was going to be broadcast continuously in my lifetime. I was wary that the future of this series would hinge on the viewing figures that the show received. So, in my paranoia, I had rushed upstairs and tuned both my cruddy television and the portable one my parents had in their bedroom to BBC One in an attempt to do my little bit to prevent the show suffering in the ratings as it had towards the end of its run in the 1980s. The Doctor was back and I didn't want him going anywhere again!

And then we heard the words 'Christopher Eccleston is the new...DOCTOR WHO!' at which point our 32" goggle-box suddenly exploded into an electric blue time vortex. The drum beat was booming, the visuals were swirling and that ancient and forever theme tune boomed into our living room. It was mesmerising to see the TARDIS falling through time and us with it. I was slightly disappointed that the Doctor's face wasn't included in this brilliant new title sequence but then I wondered whether the new audience this show was trying to find would think that idea was a little niche.

Straight away, I drew comparisons with the opening panning shot of the moon in *Spearhead From Space*. The crash zoom into Rose Tyler's dishevelled room and the subsequent documenting of that day in her slightly monotonous life, showed that, along with the title of the episode, this new series was going to be all about the companion. It was imperative that the audience found a friend in the show and Rose Tyler was that conduit. In the next 45 minutes, we discovered how pretty, resourceful and above all, normal she was. She was the perfect character to aspire to be like because she was just like us and that made her special.

It's no exaggeration to label *Rose* the most important story in Doctor Who's long and illustrious history since that brilliant and eerie first broadcast of *An Unearthly Child*. It was grounded in realism. Gone were the old power stations of the Home Counties and the far-flung space stations of yesteryear. This show was tied to recognisable surroundings and famous landmarks and it was relatable. The vast majority of those watching dreamt of nothing else but an escape from their daily lives and this new show was their chance as much as it was Rose Tyler's.

I instantly looked up to Christopher Eccleston's interpretation of the Doctor. He was funny, serious, alien and everyman all at once, revealing that lots of planets have a north and pointing out that his ears were slightly larger than he expected (I squealed with delight at this hint that he'd recently regenerated). But what sold it for me was that beautiful moment when he took Rose's hand and eloquently explained to her who he was and what they represented, clinging to the skin of this tiny planet. Despite the uncouth garb and the cropped hairstyle, this was unquestionably the man I had watched hold the future of the Daleks in his hands, open the tombs of the Cybermen and save countless civilisations with no mention of a thank you. He was the Doctor. And he had me with his first word…run!

CHILD OUT OF TIME

As Rose ran in slow motion towards the waiting TARDIS and that familiar screech penetrated our ears, I was completely sold on this new version of *Doctor Who*, as were my sisters who had been gripped throughout the proceeding three quarters of an hour. We had all fallen in love with it, as had the 10.83 million who had been watching. The show had been a resounding overnight success. Any of those lingering doubts that it would crash and burn and fall out of favour quickly with the public were soundly put to bed. In the next morning's paper, I scoured the pages to read the reviews. Not one negative word blemished those pages and the news that a Christmas special and a second series had already been confirmed was utterly glorious. The BBC's gamble had worked; *Doctor Who* was back and better than ever!

Then came the shattering headline that Christopher Eccleston was not going to continue with the series. It was crushing but in a way, it made his Doctor that more precious. We were only going to have another twelve episodes in his company so I was going to make sure that I savoured each and every one of them before the new actor came in. And of course, it meant that a regeneration was coming. That brilliant, scary invention that a thousand alchemists could never realise. There was so much to look forward to.

For the next three months, *Doctor Who* was event television for us. Each and every Saturday, there we were, taking our places for yet another adventure. And this first series of the new run was flowing with emotional depth, frightening moments, convincing effects and, above all, truly award winning acting and writing. The formula had worked and this show wasn't going to be going anywhere for a good while yet.

Suddenly, school bus journeys were accompanied by children openly discussing what they thought of the episode. It seemed like everybody was talking about *Doctor Who* now, which shocked me to my core.

For so long, this programme had almost been my dirty little secret. My hidden love. To be in the presence of my peers openly discussing how brilliant the Dalek episode was, theorising upon what the Time War might have been like and whether farting Slitheens was a good idea was more alien to me than a trip to the planet Raxacoricofallapatorius! And yet I glowed with golden energy as the warmth and love of the show from others washed my inhibitions clean. I could now come out as a *Doctor Who* fan to my friends. They would even understand if I didn't come out Saturday evening until 7.45 because they were now sharing exactly what I was doing. Bums planted on the sofa (though not behind it at our ages), watching the adventures of the Doctor, Rose, Captain Jack and Mickey, thoroughly engrossed by every single second.

CHILD OUT OF TIME

In the summer of 2005, I fell in love with *Doctor Who* all over again. And it felt fantastic!

CHAPTER TEN
JARVIS COCKER IN SPACE

I felt like I was walking in some kind of dream land. As though the matrix in my mind had sculpted a fantasy world in which my favourite show was suddenly the nation's favourite show. For 13 weeks, *Doctor Who* was the only TV programme any of us could talk about. I even remember catching a glimpse of what appeared to be a 'best-of' trailer that aired at the end of the series, which culminated in the departure of the much-loved Christopher Eccleston and the arrival of the Tenth Doctor, David Tennant.

My peers were initially sniffy about the latest incumbent in the TARDIS. I distinctly recall one of the girls on the bus (whose name will not be mentioned for her own protection) who stood up and exclaimed that 'I hate the new Doctor. That man with his stupid grin. He looks like a weasel! There's no way I'm ever watching him. He'll never be as good as Eccleston!'

Within a year, however, that girl, along with so many others, would come to love and embrace Tennant's manic portrayal of the Time Lord. And yet I struggled to pledge allegiance to an incarnation that the TV comedian and impressionist Phil Cornwell once described as 'Jarvis Cocker in Space.' For a start, he had pinched my look. Despite my tender age of 16, I had been shaving for the past few years and had already developed the ability to sprout sideburns. My haircut of preference was also long on the top, short on the back and sides, with my fringe straggling down over my eyebrows whilst the rest stood on end on top. Somehow and somewhere, the *Doctor Who* production team had seen my style and thought, 'that'll do'.

So much happened for me on a personal level during that long wait between Series One and Two. A whole summer of exploration awaited and I threw myself into the mixer of teenage abandon. My village may have been small but it was by no means boring. As we lived in a catchment area that included not one but three secondary schools of choice, the parents of Steeple Bumpstead were spoilt as to where to send their offspring for the next step in their education. So, the whole village was littered with sixteen to eighteen year-olds who multiplied as their friends ventured down from neighbouring villages for the weekend. It was as though the whole village succumbed to an invasion more terrifying than that of a Dalek or Cybermen takeover. This was an occupation of hormonal, experimental teenagers. For three days a week, this quiet little English village became party central. If you hadn't been invited to a house party, then you were not with the gang. So many people, so many stories, so many firsts and so many new friendships were made.

As we lived in a settlement that was not even equipped with its own enforcer of the law, we roamed free in the countryside. Impromptu raves would be attended by a dozen or so intoxicated friends as we would party long into the night. As I look back now, the Summer of 2005 seems like it went on forever. I can't even remember when the summer really ended!

It was at this time that I took up my first paid job as a kitchen porter in my local pub. It was a brave new world for me, a million miles away from the one I'd grown up in.

Despite my loathing of school, I had somehow achieved the gold standard of five A to C grades, which allowed me entrance into the Sixth Form at my school. However, apart from the luxury of wearing my own clothes and throwing off the conformist shackles of the school uniform and choosing my own lessons, my situation hadn't changed. I felt victimised by my peers and teachers, sometimes with good reason. So, within a year, after some terrible AS Level results, I packed in Sixth Form and started afresh at Cambridge Regional College, enrolling in a plumbing course that gave me time to figure out what I wanted to do with my life as well as develop essential skills that would eventually ensure that I'd never have to pay out for someone to fix my toilet for me.

Having longed for *Doctor Who* action figures for so many years, when they were finally on the shelves of every shop in the land, I felt that seventeen was too old for toys. Especially ones I would have been expected to pay for myself out of my hard earned cash or Education Maintenance Allowance. The scanty funds I had were only just covering my beer money and an occasional new Xbox game. So, all of this wonderful new merchandise was passing me by, taking second place to a more active social life. Could it be that my dream of *Doctor Who* returning was going to come true just as I was growing out of it? Irony of ironies!

Before long, *Doctor Who* was back. After the show's first bona fide Christmas special in *The Christmas Invasion*, the Doctor and Rose returned in *New Earth*. To be honest, I wasn't completely enamoured by this new TARDIS team. It seemed to me that this new Doctor, who was already a hit with the ladies I spoke to, was slightly too human for my liking. And the dynamic had well and truly changed between him and his 19-year-old companion from one of friendship to something much more. And when you're telling stories about a centuries-old alien, with wisdom and intellect beyond anything we mere mortals could ever dream of, I thought it was a very bad move.

Ask any *Doctor Who* fan and they will tell you that, throughout their time as a fanatic, there is always one Doctor/companion partnership that just doesn't work for them and clouds their judgment of those stories they are involved in. Despite the nostalgic glory of *School Reunion*, the heart warming yet heartbreaking *The Girl in the Fireplace*, the dark and brilliant *The Impossible Planet/The Satan Pit* and the bombastic fan's wet dream that was *Army of Ghosts/Doomsday*, I just wasn't investing in the Doctor/Rose dynamic. I kept watching, of course, as I was still concerned that, if all the televisions in our house were not tuned to BBC One, then somehow it would be my fault if the programme was cancelled again - even if the show was a resounding success.

Despite my indifference towards this new Doctor and new era for my beloved show, I still had cause to like David Tennant's interpretation. I enjoyed his cheeky, confident manner and the way that, although he was young in body, there was a galaxy-weary manner in which he dispatched the likes of the Krillitanes and took on Satan himself. The 900-year-old Time Lord was breaking through. But, as Charlie Brooker once described him, he was slightly mawkish and childlike. Not in the way that the great Patrick Troughton had been, but more in the way of a petulant younger sibling. Although I didn't shed a tear when Rose said what appeared to be her final goodbye to her Doctor on Bad Wolf Bay, I was incensed by Catherine "am I bovvered?" Tate's sudden appearance in a wedding dress aboard the TARDIS. Did this mean that she would be the next companion? I kept watching.

As Series 3 dawned in 2007, I was coming to the end of my plumbing studies. I'd made headway with my tests and practical examinations, so I finished my work in April. Just around the time that the Doctor was to return, not with the mouthy Runaway Bride, Donna, but with the medical student, Martha Jones. I wanted to approach Freema Agyeman's new character as though she was a blank canvass and give her all the chances I could to make up for what I saw as a woeful evolution to Billie Piper's turn as Rose Tyler.

On the whole, I really enjoyed Series 3. I loved *The Shakespeare Code* and, although *Daleks in Manhattan/Evolution of the Daleks* fell rather flat, *Gridlock* was an understated treasure and more than made up for a less than triumphant return of the metal monsters from Skaro. Despite Saturday nights becoming the centre of my social life, I didn't miss a single episode on original broadcast and always backed it up with domestic video recordings. Occasionally, I did purchase the DVD box-sets, as well as replacing my VHS collection with more up-to-date DVDs. I distinctly remember walking into WHSmith in Bury St Edmunds and seeing a whole host of *Doctor Who* DVDs for a relatively low price. In scenes reminiscent of my younger self snatching up every *Doctor Who* book I could find in the local library, I scooped up a menagerie of DVDs and ended up shelling out a grand total of £50 on such wonderful titles as *The Aztecs*, *Tomb of the Cybermen*, *Pyramids of Mars*, *The Talons of Weng-Chiang*, *Earthshock*, *The Caves of Androzani*, *Revelation* and *Resurrection of the Daleks*, *The Curse of Fenric* and *Survival*. I also treated myself to a six-disc pack that was exclusive to Amazon containing six classic Jon Pertwee stories, including the brilliant *Inferno*, which I'd never seen but which remains a personal favourite to this day. So, all in all, you could say the *Doctor Who* bug had well and truly bitten me again.

As my eighteenth birthday loomed, I was looking forward to what I hoped would be the best year of my life so far. And it couldn't have got off to a better start. I'd spent my Christmas bonus on tickets to my very first rock gig. And what a belter it was. A friend and I were to witness the very first rock concert at the new Wembley Stadium on June 17th 2007 and even better, it was to see one of our favourite bands, Muse. But in the build-up to these momentous events, I was to completely fall in love with *Doctor Who* all over again in the space of three weeks when three of the greatest episodes the show has ever made were broadcast back-to-back; *Human Nature/The Family of Blood* and *Blink*. They were so captivating that they inspired me to write again. I searched out those ancient files from under my bed and pored over my scribblings from previous years. These three stories had woken something in my imagination. And all it needed was a story set on the cusp of the First World War, with the Doctor converting himself into a human to hide from a deadly race out to steal his regenerations. It was a brilliantly written story unfolding over two episodes, the latter feeling like an intimate character dissection of what really makes the Doctor so great. And one line got my love for the show burning again: 'He's like fire and ice and rage. He's like the night and the storm in the heart of the sun. He's ancient and forever. He burns at the centre of time and can see the turn of the universe and... he's wonderful.'

Those words uttered by Timothy Latimer would go on to reinvigorate my creative juices. That very week, I started writing again. Not just short stories this time, but poems, lyrics and haikus. It couldn't have been a coincidence. This eloquent summing up of the character I'd looked up to for so many years was so joyous that I could have cried. To have it in one of the greatest stories of all time, which was then followed by the greatest Nu-Who story of all time in *Blink*, left me submerged in the world of Who in a way I had thought impossible after falling out of love with it in my teenage years.

Around this time, I also met and started dating someone who would become my first girlfriend who had no problems embracing my love of the show and dispelling any lingering thoughts in my mind that chicks didn't dig Time Lords. Yet sadly, it was with her that I was to experience one of my worst moments as a fan.

In mid-June, a couple of weeks after my birthday, one of my girlfriend's friends had invited us all over for a house party at his gaff in Saffron Walden, Essex. After stocking up on booze and nibbles, we all gathered around his television set for the Series 3 finale, *The Last of the Time Lords*. The penultimate episode, *The Sound of Drums*, had set the climax up nicely. The Master, now back in the guise of the wonderfully mad John Simm (who had become one of my favourite actors after his portrayal as the time travelling Sam Tyler in the brilliant *Life on Mars*) had captured the Doctor, humiliated him by ageing him into an old man and taken over the Earth with the help of the mysterious Toclafane. Only Martha Jones stood between total victory and failure.

Sadly, *Last of the Time Lords* was almost the moment I gave up completely on *Doctor Who*. I hated it and so did my peers, who laughed and pointed for 45 minutes at the TV screen, highlighting every imperfection. How they giggled when the Master pranced around to the god-awful track from Scissor Sisters. How they spat out their whiskey and cokes when the rogue Time Lord aged his old adversary into a version of Dobby the House Elf from *Harry Potter*. This finale was truly laughable. And what was worse is that I wasn't bowing to peer pressure from my friends. I really did think it was terrible and an awful waste of what had been a very good series up until then.

My worst fears had also been realised regarding the Doctor's relationship with Martha. Despite a good, solid start, the new companion had descended into having little more than a schoolgirl crush on the Doctor and it ruined her chance to develop into a great companion in my eyes. Also, to have the Doctor repeatedly saying how much he missed Rose didn't really give her much of a chance to grow in what had become an unrequited love story. I took solace in those parts of Series 3 which I had enjoyed and thought that, until Tennant's Doctor found an older, more mature travelling companion, one that wouldn't fall in love with him like Rose, Martha or even Captain Jack, I would have to revert to being a casual viewer again.

My plan to take my fandom down a notch didn't last long, however, as I got my wish as soon as Series 4 started. The character of Donna

Noble might not have left a great impression in her one-off appearance, but how she triumphed as a calming influence on David Tennant's Doctor, inspired one of the best TARDIS teams, in my opinion. Sadly, her tearful departure created what I saw as the emo-Doctor; a self-pitying, heartbroken man bearing more than the weight of the entire universe on his shoulders.

It didn't surprise me one bit when Tennant announced that he was to leave the show in late 2008. In fact, I was rather looking forward to it, as I liked the idea of Russell T Davies handing over the show runner role to Steven Moffat who, to my mind had contributed some of the best scripts in this new series vision of *Who*. I eagerly awaited the announcement of the new Doctor and, when Matt Smith was revealed as the Eleventh Doctor, I was so excited to see how he would do. At 26, he was to be the youngest Doctor of all time, and just seven years older than me! I had well and truly had enough of the Tenth Doctor and can vividly recall watching *The End of Time* with my head in my hands, whilst receiving a text from my then girlfriend who, whilst the Doctor visited all his old companions, enquired 'Has he gone yet?'

2009 was a long and drawn out year for me, much like the Tenth Doctor's demise. I had decided to pursue a career in journalism and, in doing so, had given up my sales assistant job in nearby Saffron Walden. Instead I had taken up writing as my chosen profession. The creative juices flowing within my brain had given me ambition and hope for a career in which I could develop my skills in a six-month course that might lead to bigger and better things. It was a brand new start for me and, at the age of 20, I had a new-found vigour to do the best I could. No longer were my scribbles hidden away in drawers and under my bed. Now my ideas were uploaded to my Facebook profile and I also discovered an online blog that I could keep. Avenues were opening up in front of me and, just as one Doctor changed into another, my life was about to become more involved with *Doctor Who* than it ever had been before.

CHAPTER ELEVEN
FULL CIRCLE

After I graduated from my journalism course in early 2010, I was sent out into the big wide world and decided that, if I was going to become successful in my chosen field, I would do my utmost to obtain commissions in topics that I loved. One of my first ports of call was The Doctor Who Appreciation Society which I'd rediscovered after moving some dusty old videos around in my room. Their contact details were always printed in the bottom left-hand-corner of the VHS sleeves and, having already discovered that their fanzine, *Celestial Toyroom*, was still going strong, I submitted an article called *The Gallifrey Globe Trotters* in the hope of grabbing the attention of then Editor, Tony Jordan.

The article was a marriage between my two loves, *Doctor Who* and football. Given that there were eleven incarnations to choose from, I decided to build a football team out of all of the Doctors and run through all of their positions and how they fitted with their persona. I had the small and tricky Seventh Doctor on the wing, the tough, no nonsense Ninth in defence and the flamboyant Third Doctor somewhere in midfield, taking up the mantle of the star of the team in a way that would have made George Best's antics look mild by comparison. Despite being a bonkers creation, the originality of my piece impressed the editor and I started writing for *CT* every month for the next three years, with my last regular article appearing in their 50th anniversary special. And that wasn't to be my only involvement with the show that year.

Although I was writing for *CT*, I was finding it very difficult to find work elsewhere. And yet, through the fantastic fan websites and blogs, I was able to write at will about all manner of topics to do with *Doctor Who* and, through that, I was delighted to find an outlet for my passion. Through my association with the DWAS, I even started to attend conventions and began to enjoy them more than I ever thought I could. Gone were my inhibitions of yesteryear and, now that being a fan of *Doctor Who* and science fiction fan in general was no longer seen as a cult interest, I could meet fellow fans en masse and many of those who, through the magic of the show, helped shape my childhood.

It was at my very first DWAS event, *Time 4* in late 2010, that the convention bug really bit me. Here, I was honoured to stand in the presence of the great Terrance Dicks and share a cider with this scribe of my youth and debate the merits of the new series as a whole. I then stumbled into Andrew Cartmel, who kindly allowed me to sit with him as he signed copies of his latest book and later fell into a photo session with Sylvester McCoy, whom I upset when I informed him that it was his seventh incarnation that was the current incumbent of the TARDIS when I was born. In my drunken stupor, for which I still blame Terrance Dicks, I beckoned Sylv towards me and gave him a big hug before posing for a picture that to this day still makes me smile. It took me quite a while to come down from that experience.

After several conventions, I started to take more of an active role in their set-up and in helping the guests at such events, most of which were located at the grand old Riverside Studios. I felt flushed with privilege every time I stepped into that wonderful building in Hammersmith, London. As more events came and went, I spent more time with fans, actors, writers and directors and always struggled to control my awe for them. And what memories I have. Sitting outside in the scorching summer sun with the likes of William Russell, Carole Ann Ford, Waris Hussein, Frazer Hines and Anneke Wills. Giants of the small screen! Sitting with Peter Purves for what felt like an eternity talking about our love of Tottenham Hotspur Football Club whilst others were waiting to obtain the *Blue Peter* legend's autograph. Chatting to Colin Baker in the green room that used to be home to the main set from which Chris Evans presented the ultimate Britpop entertainment show, *TFI Friday*. All the time, reminding myself how lucky I was to be there.

As the Doctor's fiftieth birthday loomed large, I had been an active member of fandom for almost three years. Still struggling for work, I had almost given up my dream of having a creative input into the show itself. I had written to many publications, submitted reviews weekly to *DWM* during Matt Smith's first series, sent story ideas to BBC Books and Big Finish but all to no avail, no matter how kind and courteous the responses were. Then, suddenly from nowhere came a bolt from the blue that would thrust me right into the eye of the storm.

Like many others, I was spellbound by the Eleventh Doctor and his feisty, red-headed assistant, Amy Pond. To me, the fifth and sixth series of Nu-Who were some of the best output the show had ever produced and this new fairytale vision from Steven Moffat was an instant favourite in our household. Still living at home, I was able to enjoy the stories with my family and even embarked on two trips to the Doctor Who Experience when it opened in Kensington Olympia in 2011. With the TARDIS team fully formed by the addition of Arthur Darvill's wonderful portrayal of Rory Williams, I had truly found my own era of the show, the one I identified with most. From now on, Matt Smith was MY Doctor. His youthful excitement, along with his sage and timeless temperament, combined for me all the best bits of my favourite classic Doctors, Patrick Troughton and Tom Baker. His alien performances delighted me week after week in the early 2010s and, even after Gillan and Darvill had moved on to be replaced by the lovely Jenna Louise Coleman, this was a Doctor I wanted to remain in charge of the TARDIS for a long time.

And then, one sunny day in early June, came the shock news that he would in fact be leaving. But it wasn't through BBC News that I learnt of Smith's decision.

I was in the bathroom when my mobile phone sparked into life beside me. Hesitantly, as this was an unknown number, I picked up and greeted my mysterious caller. 'Hello, is that Hayden Gribble?'

It was the programme co-ordinator of *BBC Breakfast*, the early-morning news programme that has broadcast daily on BBC One for the last three decades. I began to think that this was a prank call. But she said that she'd been given my number by the editor of Doctor Who Online (to which I'd contributed a few articles the previous year). This was no wind up.

'We would like you to come up to Salford and join the presenters on the red sofa and talk about Matt Smith's decision to leave Doctor Who.'

I couldn't utter a word. My head was swimming with questions. Why is Matt leaving, in the anniversary year of all years? Why would they ask me? Who was I to fandom? Was Toby Hadoke busy or something?

I stuttered my way through the conversation, scarcely believing what was happening. I was being asked to represent my favourite ever TV show which had more of an impact on my life than any other obsession. Why me? It was going to be live telly. I would have to travel up to Manchester that very night ready for transmission in the morning and keep the announcement a secret until 10pm that evening. It was a wrench to tell her that I was unemployed and so had no means of travelling up North that night.

Hanging up the conversation, I sat forlorn that I'd lost what would probably be my only chance to appear on national television. Then the phone rang again. This time, it was the editor of BBC Radio Five Live, asking whether I could attend their studios in Cambridge and speak about the very same news item at 7 o' clock the next morning. I happily accepted and sprinted downstairs to inform my family that I was to appear on radio instead.

So, as the news broke of Matt Smith's departure, I turned in for the night, my phone aglow with messages from friends. But I stayed as tight lipped as I could, posted an ambiguous message on my Facebook wall about speaking about the show on the radio the next day and proceeded to not sleep and think over and over in my head what I was going to say the next morning.

Before long, the sun was up and I was in my ancient red Ford Fiesta making the short trip to the BBC Radio Cambridgeshire studio. As it was only radio, I arrived unshaved and with my hair unmanaged and gave my name at Reception.

Within moments, I was sitting in a small room all by myself, linked in with headphones in front of a microphone protruding from a bank of cables and wires. I was to be connected to Broadcasting House where the *Five Live Breakfast Show* was transmitting live. The butterflies left my stomach as soon as the neon red "live" button flashed in front of me and I took part in a lively and fun chat with the show's presenters. It went very well, except for the moment when they confused my choice as the next Doctor, Tom Hiddleston, with the Spurs and England midfielder, Tom Huddlestone!

As I left that tiny room and passed the reception hall on my way out, the woman at the desk called me over as someone was on the other end of the phone who wanted to talk to me. I was hoping it would be Steven Moffat himself, calling to congratulate me and offer the chance as show runner for next year's series.

It wasn't the head honcho of Doctor Who but the editor of BBC News who wanted to ask whether I would consider going on live television after all to give my opinions to newscaster Nicholas Owen in an hour's time. Naturally, I jumped at the opportunity. I was to appear with a backdrop of Kings College, Cambridge (which, of course, is where Tom Baker and Lalla Ward enjoyed a punt in *Shada*) and converse through an ear piece with the famous newsreader about Matt Smith's decision to leave and who I would favour as his replacement. But, as I handed the receiver back to the receptionist, anxiety washed over me.

I realised that my dishevelled attire was not suitable for live television. I was going to be watched by thousands, maybe millions of people, including friends and family, all judging my opinions and appearance. With not a moment to waste, I told the receptionist that I would be back in a moment and headed out to buy a shaving kit and some hair gel. Like my appearance on radio, I was aware that I didn't want to come across as a stereotypical "nerd", my vanity was almost taking over the excitement of my appearance altogether.

After sprucing myself up in the Gents, I returned to the front desk, where an engineer showed me to the room I would be making my broadcast from. It was far removed from the glitz and glamour one would expect from a corporation as renowned as the BBC. Its outside dimensions incongruous with the inside. Like a reverse TARDIS, it was smaller than the room I had sat in for my radio appearance. What's more, the room was pitch black with nothing but a blank, white backdrop and a vast camera, complete with LED trim emitting a thick red light. I sat in the chair provided, facing the camera whilst the engineer supplied me with an ear piece. I carefully placed my wallet, keys and phone on the stool next to me as I was nervous of my possessions sliding out of my pockets live on air.

The engineer counted me in with a test run just minutes before transmission then suddenly began to feverishly fiddle with the sound bank to the left of the camera. There was no sound coming out of my ear piece and although the small microphone attached to my fleece was working and the editor of BBC News could hear me, I couldn't hear them.

It turned out that the sound bank was broken and my chances of making an appearance on live television started to disappear. I stayed as calm as could be but, as the news team moved onto another story, I thought my opportunity had gone. Then, to my surprise, the engineer asked me to take the ear piece out and gave me his iPhone and headset and hastily arranged a live audio link-up through his phone. He gestured to me to try to hide the white headphones by curling them behind my ears and putting the phone in my back pocket. Suddenly, the LED trim turned a brilliant green and I was live on air.

On reflection, I think I gave a pretty good account of myself. I rhapsodised about how good I thought Smith had been in the role, how he had harnessed the best of his predecessors to make the part of the Doctor his own, answered the age-old question of whether the next actor to play the part should be a woman and gave my opinion on who the next Doctor should be.

In no time at all, my fifteen minutes of fame was over and I left BBC Radio Cambridgeshire and proceeded home, my phone buzzing like mad with texts, messages and phone calls from people expressing their delight at how well I'd done. What had surprised me most about the whole experience was not the adrenaline rush of live broadcasting nor the surreal nature of speaking to people through modern technology and actually stringing together coherent sentences throughout, it was the fact that, despite there being a box in the corner of the television screen clearly saying LIVE, people will still phone you. Out of the corner of my eye whilst on TV, I could see my phone lighting up like Blackpool Illuminations!

So, already 2013 had been a rather special one for me and the surprises were not to end there.

A couple of months later, I attended *Project Motormouth 2* with a couple of friends at the Copthorne Hotel in Slough. The event was a charity fundraiser, organised by Tegan Jovanka herself, Janet Fielding, in collaboration with Tenth Planet Events. The guest list was highly impressive. A Doctor in the person of Peter Davison, a multitude of companions and a list of writers that had me salivating. It was a chance to meet stars I'd never met before, add to my autograph collection and catch up with good friends.

After a liquid lunch with my friends Jamie and John, we queued for our chance to obtain the Fifth Doctor's autograph. Whilst we had been sitting outside the hotel a little earlier, soaking up the August sunshine, we had witnessed a camera crew in BBC badges and lanyards, filming Davison pulling up to the hotel entrance in a clapped -out green Skoda. We knew it was the 50th year, so we thought it was the Beeb filming a documentary. But as we stood near the front of the queue, a member of the crew told us that we were going to be filmed for a Doctor Who project due to be transmitted later on in the year! Naturally, we were all intrigued and very excited. I thought to myself what a lucky man I was to potentially appear in something connected with Doctor Who for the second time in a couple of months. There was no direction for what we were doing and a skeleton crew, led by Davison's daughter and David Tennant's wife, Georgia Tennant, filmed me and several others queuing for Peter's signature. Like the BBC News experience, it was an odd thing to be a part of but I still managed to obtain a picture with my first TV Doctor.

However, my day was to take another surreal turn. Not an hour had passed before another unknown caller rang me out of the blue. It was the editor of BBC News again, informing me that the identity of the new Doctor was to be revealed in a top secret programme that had been set up by the BBC over the last month for live broadcast the following day. They wanted me to make the trip to Cambridge again and give my opinions on the actor (whoever it was) the day after.

Unfortunately, I had to tell them that I was unavailable for interview and, two days later, I sat down to watch *BBC Breakfast* and saw *DWM* editor Tom Spilsbury do the media rounds on the new Doctor, *The Thick of It* star Peter Capaldi. I didn't begrudge him though. He was far more qualified than me to talk about the big news.

Like everyone else, I watched the live show with bated breath to see who the new Doctor might be. I cringed throughout at the concept but enjoyed seeing my first glimpse of the Twelfth Doctor.

2013 was like one big party for *Doctor Who* fans. We were spoiled with a deluge of TV, audio, novella and non-fiction outputs that celebrated a show that, just eight years previously, had been seen by many as a gamble. The joys of *Doctor Who* just kept on coming. Not only did we have the promise of a 50th anniversary special, reuniting David Tennant and Billie Piper with the show and a mysterious unknown incarnation of the Doctor in the guise of John Hurt, but Mark Gatiss's docu-drama on the genesis of *Doctor Who*, *An Adventure in Space and Time* and then, one day in October, the promise of previously missing episodes returning to the BBC.

I had heard rumblings throughout fandom for a couple of years that someone had discovered long-lost stories in Africa, and it wasn't until I interviewed a well-respected person at the British Film Institute in June 2013 that I had it confirmed to me that something was coming back. It was back at the BFI, attending a meeting regarding missing television shows, that I discovered the brilliant news that two Patrick Troughton adventures were back, and that one of them was *The Web of Fear*, that brilliant base-under-siege tale that had gripped my imagination as a child through the power of its Target novel.

But these nuggets of gold were nothing compared to what I experienced on the week of the anniversary. I don't think television has made me cry tears of joy more than those I shed when watching the specials. I welled up when Matt Smith appeared as a vision to David Bradley's stunning interpretation of William Hartnell at the very end of the fantastic *An Adventure in Space and Time*. I yelped and cheered at almost every minute of *The Day of the Doctor* and punched the air when every single incarnation of the Time Lord (including Capaldi) saved Gallifrey. I sat, my mouth open in shock at Tom Baker's triumphant cameo at the end. I can't criticise either special, they were both glorious love letters to a show that has given me so much.

On the evening of 23rd November 2013, I accompanied a few fellow fans to our local village pub to discuss what we had just seen. There was still the anticipation of Matt Smith's final adventure on Christmas Day but, apart from that, 2013 had one further surprise in store for me.

I walked away from the bar, whiskey and coke in hand, and checked my texts. To my surprise, I had several in my inbox including two from my mother, informing me that I had just been on TV again. I couldn't think what it might have been in and then I twigged it. I was taken back in my mind to the Copthorne Hotel in August and the bizarre events in that room with Peter Davison, a camera crew and several other unwitting fans. Without knowing it, I'd appeared as an extra in a spoof called *The Fiveish Doctors Reboot*. When I returned home, there I was, peeping over the shoulder of my friend. I re-watched the special over and over again on iPlayer, taking repeated screenshots of myself and posting them on social media. I was so proud to have made a tiny contribution to the celebrations. Through a couple of live appearances, countless articles for CT and a turn as an extra, I felt like I had given something back to the show that had given me so much happiness throughout my life.

And now, things have come full circle. I remain active in fandom as a writer and podcaster but little has changed. I am still that seven-year-old boy, writing short stories about my favourite character and hero and talking about it with fellow fans. Every now and again, I treat myself to a day out at a convention and pinch myself when being given the chance to stand next to the people who have made *Doctor Who* the success it always will be. To sit in my living room and look up at framed pictures of myself with Tom Baker, Peter Davison, Colin Baker, Sylvester McCoy and Peter Capaldi fills me with enormous pride and memories that will live with me forever.

After nearly twenty years since that fateful day in the old folk's home in Warwickshire, I look back and forward to my life with the Doctor and can only think of two words to sum it all up. What luck!

What luck to have been able to write so many loving articles for Doctor Who publications. What luck to have met so many wonderful friends and the people who have helped bring Doctor Who to life over its 54 year history.

What luck to have sat in the BFI on the Southbank amongst a whole host of super fans and learn that two almost complete stories from the Patrick Troughton era, *The Enemy of the World* and *The Web of Fear* were being returned to the BBC nearly 45 years after their first broadcast. And what luck to sit there a few months later in the company of the actors who contributed to those classics in the Prince Charles cinema in Leicester Square, London and watch them in their full restored glory. What luck to meet Tom Baker not once but twice and speak to a man who to me is like the stars in the night sky; distant, magnificent and always there.

What luck to be asked to join a bi-weekly podcast like the *Diddly Dum Podcast* back in February 2015 and, alongside other enthusiastic fans, the effervescent Doc Whom, Mark John and Allan Lear, get the chance to broadcast our own views, features, interviews and embrace the show we love with fellow fans new and old.

And what luck to be at that impressionable age on the eve of a false dawn in the Doctor's real-life timeline and clasp that show so tightly to my heart, at a time when it was unloved by the masses and for it to feel so special to me, the boy that was whisked away by a Time Lord in a blue Police Box.

Doctor Who changed my life. I cannot underestimate its influence throughout my life and the effect it has had on me, for the better. Even now, on a cold winter's night, I'll still reach for one of those old Target novelisations or a battered, sun bleached VHS copy of a story broadcast so far back in the mists of time that teary-eyed nostalgia just about does it justice. Even though I love the regeneration of the show in the 21st century, nothing beats a bit of classic *Doctor Who* every now again.

What can I say? I am a child out of time, after all…

ACKNOWLEDGEMENTS

I'd like to say a big thank you to the following people for helping me get this book out of my head and on to the page. Andrew Smith, Una McCormack, Paul Magrs, Dave Probert, Matthew Kilburn, Ian Wheeler, Grant Bull, Peter Ware, Jamie Wells, Phil Newman, Dave Greenham, Tony Jordan, Paul Winter, the Doctor Who Appreciation Society, my lovely girlfriend Sophie, my family and last but not least my Diddly Dum co-conspirators Steve Hayward, Mark John and Allan Lear. Your encouragement, sage advice and wise counsel went a long way.

ABOUT THE AUTHOR

Hayden Gribble was born in the summer of 1989. He spent his formative years absorbing the television of yesteryear through repeats of the Gerry Anderson Supermarionation series, *Doctor Who*, *The Simpsons*, *Red Dwarf* and *Dad's Army*. He was also mesmerised by the *James Bond* film series and the action cartoons of the late 1980s and early 1990s.

As adulthood dawned, he had tried to pass himself off as an adult by writing for a number of publications such as the Doctor Who Appreciation Society newszine, *Celestial Toyroom*, music writer for *B-Side Magazine*, Features and Vortextra contributor to *Doctor Who Online* and working as a football writer for *goal.com* and *Eurosport*.

In 2014, he wrote and self-published his first novel, *The Man in the Corner*. He followed this up with a collection of poems and lyrics from his teenage years called *Tales From Another Me*, released as a kindle book in 2015.

He appears regularly on the *Diddly Dum Podcast* and, since 2016, has hosted his own show, *Podcasters Royale: The James Bond 007 Show*.

Find Hayden on Twitter @gribbla12
www.haydengribble.net
www.facebook.com/haydengribbleauthor

Printed in Great Britain
by Amazon